A GUIDE TO INTEGRATING TECHNOLOGY STANDARDS INTO THE CURRICULUM

Michelle Churma

Merrill,
an imprint of Prentice Hall

Upper Saddle River, New Jersey   Columbus, Ohio

Editor: Debra A. Stollenwerk
Production Editor: JoEllen Gohr
Cover Designer: Diane C. Lorenzo
Cover art: © Photodisk, Inc.
Production Manager: Pamela Bennett
Director of Marketing: Kevin Flanagan
Marketing Manager: Suzanne Stanton
Marketing Coordinator: Krista Groshong

*Lesson plans summarized and reprinted with permission of the
International Society for Technology in Education.*

Printed in the United States of America

10 9 8 7 6 5 4 3

ISBN: 0-13-974114-3

For my father...

ACKNOWLEDGMENTS

Thanks to the following people for their assistance with this book:

Peggy Roblyer, for all her work on the lesson plans.
Debbie Stollenwerk, for her assistance and patience.

PREFACE

This text is designed for educators interested in using the curriculum standards set by such organizations as the National Council of Teachers of Mathematics and the National Council for Teachers of English. It provides ideas for combining technology with these standards to create a classroom of learners prepared for the 21st century.

Descriptions of the technology-related standards are provided for Mathematics, English/Language Arts, Social Sciences, Geography, Economics and Science. Suggestions for the use of technology with the other standards are also included.

Ideas for using common technology tools in each of the subject areas provide teachers with ways to integrate technology into the standards with software usually found in the classroom. The common tools include spreadsheets, word processors, the Internet, and hypermedia tools such as *HyperStudio*.

The integration of technology into the standards is also addressed through the various lesson plans presented in the text. These lesson plans were collected and linked to the standards in a searchable database created by M. D. Roblyer (see list of suggested readings for more information).

Finally, this text presents a list of Internet and print resources to help teachers with the integration of technology into the standards.

CONTENTS

◆ SETTING THE STAGE FOR TECHNOLOGY

Overview of the Tradition

Computers and related technologies seem to be the buzzword for education as we approach the start of the 21st century. However, computers are not new to education. Computers appeared in schools in the late 1950s and early 1960s as a tool for programmed instruction. As computer technology developed, so did its use in the classroom. The 1960s saw this technology used for computer-based instruction, including tutorials on reading and mathematics. These early uses of computers usually involved connections to a mainframe computer managed by a software company, a university, or a school district office. Computer-based instruction continued through the 1970s and 1980s. With the development of microcomputers, the control of the computer became the responsibility of the classroom teacher. Even as courseware became more common, many educators began to feel that it was important to teach *about* computers and so computer literacy programs were developed. These programs had originally focused on programming and the use of common computer tools such as the word processor. Students began to use the computers to write programs, completing activities that educators hoped would allow the students to develop logical thinking skills. Students also learned word and data processing to prepare them for careers in an increasingly technological world. Computer literacy programs later began to include all sorts of computer related skills, including keyboarding (Roblyer, Edwards, & Havriluk, 1997).

The use of computers in today's classrooms seems to have returned to the idea of integration and even expanded upon it. Teachers are again viewing computer technology as something that could enhance *any* lesson they were teaching; and while basic computer skills are still taught as separate classes, integration is often the major reason for using computer technology. Drill and practice software, tutorials, simulations, and educational games are available to help students learn math skills, practice their spelling, explore the lives of pioneers and explorers and even dissect frogs. Databases and spreadsheets provide students with tools to not only record data, but, perhaps more importantly, to explore what the data may mean. The development of easy to use multimedia authoring software has allowed the computer to be used for open-ended creative projects. And, the addition of the Internet to the classroom allows students to communicate with the world as well as to explore a seemingly endless array of topics. The possibilities of educational computing in the 21st century may well be limited only by our imaginations.

The Need for Technology Integration in the Curriculum

It has been said that to be productive in the 21st century, students will need to have strong computer skills. Whether or not this is the case, schools across the nation have been increasing the amount of computers and other technologies available to their students. As the amount of technology in the schools increases, it is important that it is used wisely. Too often schools have purchased technology with no real plan for its use or integration into the curriculum. Without some sort of plan, the technology is often underused or even misused (Roblyer, Edwards, & Havriluk, 1997).

Technology that is well integrated into the classroom can, however, be of great benefit to both teachers and students. Teachers can integrate technology into the management of their classroom—for electronic gradebooks, electronic communications, word processing and other such tasks. For students, the integration of technology can help with the review of basic skills and the development of writing skills, research skills, higher order thinking skills, and creativity.

Technology may also play a role in helping to motivate students, including those students who have been labeled "at risk." It can help students focus their attention on the material at hand through a variety of characteristics, including graphics and sound, isolated displays of problems, and interactivity. It can also help students feel in control of their learning by allowing them to control the pace of the information, choose the level of problems, or even create their own materials (Roblyer, Edwards, & Havriluk, 1997).

Students also benefit from the integration of technology when it allows them to visualize problems and solutions. Visual representations of materials can help students move from concrete to abstract learning. For example, the program *The Graph Club* allows elementary students to explore the concepts of graphs by manipulating pictures on the screen and listening to the computer count the items in the graph. Items in a graph can be visualized as a line, bar or circle graph, as individual objects for students to count, and as a number, allowing students to work with the information in whatever way works best for them. Older students can use *Geometer Sketchpad* to investigate geometry concepts by manipulating shapes and exploring concepts and proofs. As they manipulate the size of angles and proportions of shapes, the students can use this program to visualize why a proof or theorem is correct.

Technology also allows students to develop problem solving and higher order thinking skills. With technology, students can move beyond focusing on basic skills such as computation and memorization and move toward applying knowledge, testing results and synthesizing information. When technology handles the basic skills, students are free to explore relationships of ideas, test hypotheses, and construct knowledge.

Introducing Standards for Technology and Education

Throughout the history of computers in the classroom, individual teachers and districts have been responsible for deciding how computers would be used in the classroom. The amount and type of computer use has depended upon the enthusiasm and training of the teachers, as well as the access to technology. As technology has become more pervasive in society and more available in the schools, educators are beginning to develop guidelines for the use of technology in the classroom. Many of the learned societies for educators have included technology requirements in their standards.

One such learned society is the National Council for Accreditation of Teacher Education (NCATE). This organization defines standards for teacher education programs throughout the United States. In many of the certification areas, NCATE demands that teacher education students at the preservice and graduate levels receive some training and/or experience with educational technology in their field of study.

Programs for preservice students in elementary education are asked to provide experiences in selecting and using appropriate technology resources for elementary students. The Initial Early Childhood program asks its preservice students to be able to evaluate technology for use with young children, to demonstrate the appropriate uses of technology with these children, and to evaluate and use assistive technology appropriate for students with disabilities.

Other NCATE approved programs also require students to develop some skills with educational technology. The Advanced Reading Education program requires its students to be able to select and use appropriate forms of educational technology in their teaching. The English/Language Arts program includes a guideline for preservice teachers to be prepared to understand non-print media and its relationship to print media and to aspects of culture, and to apply these skills in their classrooms. The mathematics guidelines require that its preservice teachers are able to use calculators and computer software to solve mathematical problems and to assist the students in their classroom to do the same (NCATE Approved Curriculum Guidelines, 1995).

The teachers graduating from these and other NCATE approved programs are required to have some technology skills. But how are these teachers going to integrate technology into their classrooms? The learned societies for many of the K–12 subject areas have provided standards for curriculum content. Many of these subject specific standards include statements on technology integration. And, even when the standards are not technology specific, there are many possibilities for the integration of educational technology into a curriculum.

◆ INTEGRATING THE STANDARDS

Mathematics

The Standards

The National Council of Teachers of Mathematics (NCTM) addresses the issue of technology integration in their standards for the K–12 math curriculum. NCTM's approach is not to identify specific technology standards, but rather, to view the integration of technology from a more global perspective. At the K–4 level, the standards suggest using computers and calculators as tools for exploring patterns, numerical ideas, and problem-solving processes. These technological tools are not to be a replacement for learning basic computation skills, but rather to help students check the results of their work, to simulate mathematical ideas, and to help students discover the key concepts of what they are learning. This approach allows students to learn to identify the appropriate times to use these technologies and also supports the goal of the Standards to avoid using pen-and-paper only activities for any extended period of time. (Curriculum and Evaluation Standards for School Mathematics, 1989).

For grades 5–8, these Standards state that students should be allowed to use computers, calculators and other technologies when appropriate. This goal is explicitly stated in Standard 7. These technologies will allow the students to shift their focus from the basic computations to problem solving and other content questions. These technologies also provide students with the opportunity to explore new mathematical content and ideas. They also give students the opportunity to explore connections and the underlying principles of mathematical concepts by allowing them to explore the effects of different values on equations, shapes, angles and other mathematical devices.

The Standards for grades 9–12 do not focus on computational skills; rather the focus is on interpretation, analysis, and exploration. Scientific calculators and computers are an important part of the Standards for grades 9–12. These tools would help support the goal of the Standards for estimation skills, judging the reasonableness of results, and problem solving. As students use technological tools to complete their calculations, the students no longer have to focus on basic skills; they can examine the larger issues and search for relationships and meanings within the information and develop the higher level thinking skills described in these standards.

Using Common Technology Tools in Math Education

Spreadsheets. One of the most common computer based tools in mathematics education is the spreadsheet. The spreadsheet can be used to solve mathematical problems, to explore the relationship of numbers, and to calculate budgets.

For example, in order to have students explore the relationship between area and perimeter, a spreadsheet could be used. Especially for younger students, the formulas for area and perimeter should already be entered into the spreadsheet. The students could then use this premade spreadsheet to enter various values for the length and width of a space. As the students explore the effects of doubling, tripling or otherwise changing values for length and width, they can discover some characteristics of area and perimeter, how they relate to the length and width of a shape, and how they relate to each other. From this exploration, students may even be able to deduce the formulas. Students could also use this spreadsheet to enter values from real objects to explore their area and perimeter. By using real objects, the students will be able to visualize the relationships of the values presented in the spreadsheet. This activity allows for the explorations of connections and underlying principles of mathematical concepts as described in the NCTM Standards for grades 5–8 as well as the standards for the exploration of mathematical concepts appropriate for all grade levels.

Internet. The Internet is another computer-based tool that is becoming more and more popular in the mathematics classroom. Students can explore information on famous mathematicians or complete math-related projects with other classrooms. Students can also find answers to their math questions, or even submit their own questions to Dr. Math. The *Ask Dr. Math* website, based at Swarthmore College, but utilizing math students from a number of other colleges, answers questions submitted by students at all grade levels. An archive of questions is available for searching, but if a student cannot find the answer to their question, they may submit it to Dr. Math via e-mail. The site also contains links to math problems, projects, and puzzles for use in all grade levels. These questions could be used as part of the curriculum or as extension activities. The *Ask Dr. Math* website address is http://forum.swarthmore.edu/dr.math. The exploration of information and the composing of mathematical questions encouraged by this site support the NCTM standards for grades K–12 of exploring mathematical concepts and communicating mathematically. The various problems may also meet other standards depending on their content.

Hypermedia. Hypermedia authoring programs such as *HyperStudio* can be used to create programs and presentations for the math classroom. For example, a hypermedia program could be used to create a step by step file on how to factor an equation in algebra. A problem can be displayed on the screen, with links to identify and explain each part of the equation. This would allow students to explore the explanations for each part of the problem as they need them. As students move through the program, each screen can present a further step in the factoring process. A help button could be available to explain terms or review previous steps. Following the screens of information, practice problems could be provided to the student, allowing them to check their work through each step of the process, and allowing them links to help and reviews on the factoring process. The completed program provides math students with the opportunity to explore factoring at their own pace.

Creating this type of program allows students to communicate mathematically, practice computation skills, and even problem solve; all of which are part of the Standards for all grade levels.

Math Lesson Plans

❖ ❖

Title: Teaching Subtraction with Graphing
Grade Level: 1–2
Source: Brehm, B., Metheny, D., Decker, C., Heidner, R. (1994). Using graphing to teach subtraction. *The Computing Teacher, 22* (3), 36–38.

Objectives/Purposes:
- Analyze and interpret information in a simple bar graph.
- Use a simple bar graph to complete simple subtraction problems with missing addends.

Young students often have trouble with subtraction problems in which they must find the missing addend, e. g., 3 + ? = 5 where students must find "how many more" must be added to equal 5. To help them solve such problems, teachers often use manipulatives to give them a concrete basis for understanding the problem. The three activities described here are designed to help young students make the transition from concrete to abstract representations of such mathematical concepts.

In the first two activities, students use graphics tools and graphing programs to create pictorial representations of the

15

problems. In the last activity, they use a drill software with a graphing component to practice their graphing and subtraction skills.

Procedures:

1. Activity #1 — Students line up in the room according to hair color to create a "human bar graph." Or the students may be asked to wear their favorite color and line up by clothing colors. They observe the number of students in each line and use a graphics program such as *Kid Pix* to make a pictograph with bars representing each color. Then the class solves "how many more" subtraction problems related to hair or clothing color (e. g., "How many more of us have brown hair than blonde hair?") by examining their pictographs.

2. Activity #2 — In the next class session, the class reviews subtraction problems using the pictographs from the first activity. The teacher introduces the activity of making a bar graph to represent the season of each child's birthday. (Seasons are used instead of months since there would not be enough entries in each month to make a good graph.) The teacher gives each student a colored rectangle representing the season of their birthday and helps the students paste their rectangle on a poster to create a bar graph. Then they use the graphing program to make a graph with bars representing each season; again they solve subtraction problems related to the graph (e. g., "How many more students were born in Spring as opposed to Summer?")

3. Activity #3 — For the final activities, they used a graphing component in Sunburst's *Muppet Math* which has Miss Piggy doing a series of exercises (e. g., jumping jacks, knee bends). The program graphs the number of each type exercise she must do. After she completes a certain number of a given exercise, the program asks the students "how many more" questions and they must analyze the graph and supply the missing number.

National Standards:
NCTM Mathematics Standards for Grades K–4
- STANDARD #1: Mathematics as problem solving
- STANDARD #6: Number sense and numeration
- STANDARD #11: Statistics and probability

Required Resources:
A math drill program with a graphing activity such as *Muppet Math* (Sunburst); a simple graphing program such as *The Graph Club* (Tom Snyder), *Exploring Tables and Graphs* (Optimum Resources), or *Easy Graph II* (Houghton Mifflin); and a graphics program such as *Kid Pix* (Broderbund) or *KidWorks* (Davidson).

❖ ❖

Title: A Chess Club by E-mail
Grade Level: 5–12
Source: Gittelson, H. (1993). The FIRN chess club. *The Florida Technology in Education Quarterly, 5*(3), 64–66.

Objectives/Purposes:
* Practice problem solving strategies and skills by playing chess via e-mail.

When two schools have a love for chess and the distance between them is great, telecommunications offers the chance to get "chess-aholics" together in an economical way. Chess has a system of notation that has long been employed to play through the mail as well as over the telephone. Computers allow instant combat over distance via e-mail. No cars, chaperones, and travel to deal with! Sparring against the same friend weekly at the school chess club is replaced by doing royal battle across the state or even across the nation by e-mail!

Reflecting life in its critical thinking and life-and-death struggles, this seemingly tame parlor game with its recreational and competitive nature is an exciting way to introduce many sound problem solving skills to youngsters. From analyzing the position to planning and executing a mating attack, kids learn the skills so critical and necessary in many other areas of school.

Depending on the mode of play (chat or e-mail messaging), matches can be of different sizes. If games are played by chat mode, a small group is best. Otherwise the games will take a very long time. Four to six games may prove best. If games are played by e-mail, then the number of games per class can be maximized because the time needed to make a response is expanded, the amount of equipment is reduced, and transmission of all moves can be made in one e-mail message. A standard time is one move per day per game for e-mail games.

Procedures:

- Prerequisites — Students need to know how to move the chess pieces and have knowledge of how to write the chess moves (chess notation). This latter skill is a nice activity to teach along with mathematical ordered pairs. Chess notation is based on moving through a grid by naming squares as an ordered pair. The teachers involved may find it helpful to create a brief player's manual that describes how to write the moves and tells the rules of playing chess by computer.

    The school in which this activity was implemented had four games going over chat mode at one time. Each class was divided into four teams (as opposed to individual vs. individual) and members were allowed to consult on each move. This way more students were able to participate and were using a cooperative effort to learn the game of chess as well as how to write the moves.

- Playing the game — Chess is not a fast activity, so games take more than one session. Ten moves per hour is a common rate of play. It may take 3 sessions of one hour to complete a game. Late afternoon/evening or Saturday sessions of 2 to 2½ hours are suggested for one-day competitions and greater parent participation. E-mail games transmitted at the rate of one move per day could take from 1 to 3 months to complete. Use the following procedures:

    1: Schools are contacted to join the E-mail Chess Club and receive the player's manual.
    2: After studying how to write the chess moves, the teachers arrange a time to connect to play a "friendly match."
    3: The classes are split into 4 teams with the roles of player, recorder, and observers.
    4: Chess boards are set up near the computer connected to e-mail for easy transmission of moves.
    5: Experts and parents are invited to help monitor and assist with games and transmissions.
    6: Make the e-mail connection.
    7: Decide who will play the white and black pieces in all games.
    8: Rounds proceed orderly with all moves for each school sent before receiving school responds with their moves. Play continues in this alternating fashion.

- Extension activities — Consider the following as follow-up activities:
    * Set up tournaments by e-mail between individuals from different schools.

* Establish chess leagues at all levels by creating a schedule of after school or Saturday dates to play matches, record results, and share games with everyone in a newsletter.

National Standards:
NCTM Mathematics Standards for Grades 5–8 and 9–12
- STANDARD #3: Mathematics as reasoning

Required Resources:
Computers set up with e-mail access; classroom or student e-mail accounts; teacher-produced chess players manual; chess boards set up in the classroom.

◆ ❤

Title: A Bottle Project for Learning about Graphs
Grade Level: 5–8
Source: Neiss, M. (1994–95). Analyzing and interpreting graphs in the middle grades—Bottles and beyond. *The Computing Teacher, 22* (4), 27–29.

Objectives/Purposes:
- Use graphs to communicate and interpret numerical information.
In this activity, students do a hands-on experiment with bottles to learn how to use graphs to communicate numerical information.

Procedures:
1. Preparation — Obtain the required materials: some clear glass bottles of different sizes and shapes, a graduated cylinder for measuring volume in milliliters, rule for measuring height in millimeters, and some water. Each student or small group of students gets one of the bottles. Have them use the Draw mode of an integrated software package such as *ClarisWorks* to draw a picture of their bottle. The teacher prepares a spreadsheet to display the data.
2. Hands-on experiment — Have students pour 10 ml of the water into their bottle and measure the height of the water in the bottle. The students enter the data in a spreadsheet that the teacher has prepared. Have them continue adding water in 10 ml increments, measuring the height and recording the data as they go.
3. Graphing and analyzing the data — Have students use the spreadsheet's charting mode to graph the data, and then use cut and paste to transfer the spreadsheet data and the graph to a word processing file. The teacher begins a discussion of how the

shape of the bottle relates to the graph. For example, if a bottle has straight sides, the graph is a straight line. Have them summarize what they have learned about the relationship between a bottle and the shape of the graph.

4. Analyzing "mystery bottles" — Give the students sets of data already entered in the spreadsheet and ask them to determine the shape of the bottle from the graph. Encourage students to use the term "slope" between the sets of points in their discussions. Finally, ask students to predict and sketch graphs for various shapes of bottles that have not yet been filled with water.

National Standards:
NCTM Mathematics Standards for Grades 5–8
- STANDARD #2: Mathematics as commuication
- STANDARD #4: Mathematical connections
- STANDARD #10: Statistics

Required Resources:
Integrated software package with drawing and spreadsheet software; clear glass bottles of various sizes/shapes; graduated cylinder for measuring volume in ml; ruler for measuring height in mm; and water.

♦ ♦

Title: Teaching Trigonometry with *Geometer's Sketchpad*
Grade Level: 9–12
Source: Charischak, I. (1996). Measuring heights, or what trigonometry tables are all about. *Learning and Leading with Technology, 23*(5), 13–16.

Objectives/Purposes:
- Use a clinometer to obtain data to help measure heights of objects.
- Use trigonometric formulas to help solve geometry problems involving heights.

Trigonometry is a branch of mathematics in which students often are asked to do many activities they do not understand conceptually. This activity is designed to let students use the *Geometer's Sketchpad* software to gain a better conceptual grounding in some common trigonometry principles.

During this lesson, students launch rockets and determine which one goes the highest. The students can use a "clinometer," an instrument that allows one to solve problems relating to heights that cannot be measured directly, to help solve the problem.

Procedures:
1. Preparation — Students learn how to use the clinometer by measuring an object such as a telephone pole. The teacher demonstrates how to use it by measuring off a certain distance from the pole and using the clinometer to measure the angle of elevation. Then the students take their readings and determine the clinometer reading. To check the accuracy of their figures (and their logic), the teacher asks them to draw a triangle that shows a scale drawing of the pole and indicates the angle of elevation.
2. Problem solving — After they do the drawing, they realize that the clinometer reading gave them angle ACB, not the angle of elevation, CAB, they needed. The teacher asks them to look at a "dynamic triangle" created with the *Geometer's Sketchpad* software. In this drawing, the triangle is dynamic because it can be changed by dragging the vertex to various positions. The teacher lets them experiment with this drawing to lead them to the insight: you get the angle of elevation by taking the clinometer reading and subtracting it from 90 degrees. This allows them to solve the problem with the pole.
3. Extending the utility — Since the students will not want to make a scale drawing for every rocket they send up, they want to create a method for calculating the height. The teacher helps them by creating and demonstrating to them a digital image of the pole they just measured. A QuickTake camera is used to create a pict. file of the image, which is then imported into the *Geometer's Sketchpad* software. The students realize the snapshot is a smaller version of their real drawing and that the *Geometer's Sketchpad* software can help them measure it. The teacher leads them to understand that they should use a "stretch factor" to multiply the figures in the smaller drawing to get the actual figures of the subsequent drawings. She shows them that they can do this with a tangent. Since a tangent is a line that touches a circle in one and only one place, the stretch factor can be obtained by getting the measurement of the side corresponding to the pole for any angle of elevation. She shows them how they can draw a tangent and use a Table of Tangents stored in a spreadsheet file to obtain the stretch factor.

    They do the following steps to do a dynamic drawing with the *Geometer's Sketchpad* software:

- Draw a circle with the diameter of 1 unit.
- Draw a radius AB.
- Highlight line AB and point B.
- Draw the perpendicular line, then hide the line.
- Place a point C on the line.
- Draw segments AC and BC and measure angle BAC and BC.

BC is the tangent of angle CAB. The radius BA equals 1, so the length of the baseline will be the stretch factor. Students can find any measure they need by dragging the vertex up or down until they have the desired angle. Then the length of BC (the missing side) is the length multiplied by the stretch factor. The students realize they can compare the measurements of this triangle with the values in the Table of Tangents and get a tangent length to correspond to the angle of elevation. When they multiply the tangent times the baseline length, they will have their answer.

National Standards:
NCTM Mathematics standards for Grades 9–12
- STANDARD #1: Mathematics as problem solving
- STANDARD #7: Geometry form a synthetic perspective
- STANDARD #9: Trigonometry

Required Resources:
Clinometer, *The Geometer's Sketchpad* (Key Curriculum Press) software; QuickTake camera; Table of Tangents on a spreadsheet

❖ ❖

Title: Teaching Mathematics with Computer Simulations
Grade Level: 9–12, at-risk students
Source: Leali, S. (1995). Using computer simulations with at-risk students. *Learning and Leading with Technology, 23*(2), 8–9.

Objectives/Purposes:
- Apply mathematics concepts and skills to the solution of real-life problems.
- Organize and plan financial records for activities such as budgeting and sales.

Computer simulations can help students transfer theoretical concepts of mathematics to applications in real-life situations. The activity described below uses specific simulations and targets at-risk students, but the same model could be used with other simulations and with students at many ability levels.

The programs used in this activity are from Sunburst Communications and include:

- "Hot Dog Stand" and "Comparison Shopping" (from the *Survival Math* disk) — The first lets students manage a business selling hot dogs during football games, and the second calls for them to shop for groceries from a home computer.
- "Budget for Success" (from the *Managing Lifestyles* package) — The program lets students plan a six-month budget. They have to consider factors such as salary, family size, rent, utilities, and unexpected expenses.

Procedures:
1. Daily preparation — The class is divided into small groups. Students meet each day in their cooperative groups and complete a 5–10 minute warm-up activity. Then they check their work with the teacher and go on to their daily assignment.
2. Problem-solving activities — Students use the three programs described above on alternating days. Each group decides the roles each member will play for the week. Roles include leader, observer, keyboarder, and accountant/recorder. At the end of each class period, groups should spend five minutes evaluating verbally how well they did that day and how they had worked together as a group. Also, they should establish a group goal for the next session.
3. Managing logistics — To guide their work and keep them focused, students must keep a written journal of their activities and progress. They can take turns doing the recording. The teacher should move among the groups acting as facilitator: asking questions, monitoring, and providing support where necessary. The teacher should also structure the activity so that cooperative learning can take place. Goals must be defined so that students are as concerned about the group's performance as they are about their own.

National Standards:
NCTM Mathematics Standards for Grades 5–8 and Grades 9–12
- STANDARD #1: Mathematics as problem solving
- STANDARD #4: Mathematical connections

Required Resources:
Survival Math and *Managing Lifestyles* software (Sunburst Communications) or similar software packages.
❖ ❖

❖ ❖

Title: When MicroWorlds and Real Worlds Collide
Grade Level: K–4
Source: Salisbury, D. (1995). Does Cincinnati need another bridge? *Learning and Leading with Technology, 23*(1), 17–19.

Objectives/Purposes:
* Explore geometric shapes by identifying them in real world structures.
* Do research on a topic and summarize and present findings in a multimedia format.
* Using data from real-world structures, develop multimedia simulations of bridge structures and operations.

This thematic unit is designed to show students some real-world applications of geometry by letting them use a Logo-based hypermedia software to develop a bridge-building proposal for their local community. Although this proposal is specific to the Cincinnati area, the same concept could be used to examine similar real or simulated projects in other areas.

Procedures:
The project uses the *MicroWorlds Project Builder* software, a Logo-based hypermedia package from LCSI. It has the following steps:

1. Community survey — The students begin by surveying community members about their attitudes toward a proposed new bridge across the Ohio River. With the help of the teachers, they create a spreadsheet to hold both the survey and the results.
2. Bridge studies — The class gathers background information on bridges in their community: historical documents, stories, and poems. As they study the shapes and designs of various bridges, they also explore information about geometric shapes in their mathematics class. Students begin to use drawing tools in *ClarisWorks* to draw sketches of a bridge of their choice.
3. Students then go on field trips to see the bridges they are studying. They discuss the geometric shapes they see in the bridges and why they are part of the bridge design.
4. Simulating activities — The students design their own electronic bridge simulation using the *MicroWorlds Project Builder* software. They learn to use the software, manipulating the variables of angles, ratio, length, and speed to make objects move.

They construct their own bridges, add bridge traffic, and calculate estimates of the number of people who would cross the bridge in a given period.

5. Final steps — After their design is complete, students can choose songs to accompany the simulation. To test the structural strength afforded by various geometric shapes, they can make bridge models with straws. Finally, they should compose a statement about their findings, and prepare to submit their report to the city commissioners or another group (if appropriate).

National Standards:
NCTM Mathematics Standards for grades K–4
- STANDARD #9: Geometry and spatial sense
- STANDARD #4: Mathematical connections

For grades 5–8
- STANDARD #4: Mathematical connections
- STANDARD #12: Geometry

NCTE English/Language Arts
- STANDARD #7: Students conduct research on issues and interests by generating ideas and questions and by posing problems.
- STANDARD #8: Students use a variety of technological and information resources (e. g., libraries, networks, databases, video) to gather and synthesize information and to create and communicate knowledge.

Required Resources:
MicroWorlds Project Builder (LCSI); spreadsheet; drawing/graphics program.

◆ ◆

Title: Learning Mathematics with Flight Simulators
Grade Level: 4
Source: van den Brink, J. (1994). Outside, the world goes by...Applying mathematics with flight simulators. *The Computing Teacher, 21*(5), 29–32.

Objectives/Purposes:
- Read settings on flight-simulated instruments: speedometer, altimeter, and compass.
- Calculate direction and distances by reading flight-simulated instruments.

- Design a map for a navigation plan between two locations for a simulated flight.

This lesson gets students to apply several mathematical skills in a simulation of a real-world situation. It can also be used with students in grades 5–8.

Procedures:
1. Preparation — Use one or two of the pre-programmed demonstration flights that come with the software to show students how the flight simulator works. Do a whole-class demonstration with a projection device connected to the computer. Prepare a worksheet made up of questions and problems along with each of several screen shots from the software. Assign this for a homework review to do after the demonstration.
2. Flight activities — During the "flight," the students watch the screen, read the instruments, and keep track of the readings in a logbook. Discuss the following as the flight progresses:
   - *Speed in knots*: These are in nautical miles per hour. Calculate how many kilometers per hour the speed would be.
   - *Altitude*: This is expressed in feet, but each single digit represents thousands of feet (e.g., 1 = 1000 feet, 2 = 2000 feet, etc.). There are two hands: one to indicate hundreds of feet, and one to indicate thousands. For example, if the big hand points to 1 and the small one to 6, then the altitude is 1,000 + 600 = 1,600 feet.
   - *Compass*: Since this changes with each turn it makes sense to record the directions one-by-one in a logbook.
   - *Horizon indicator*: This shows whether the plane is going up, down, or holding steady.

   Ask questions such as:
   - If the speed is 60 mph, how many kilometers per hour is that?
   - How long have we been flying?
   - How do we measure distance?
   - How many feet does the altimeter show for the altitude.
   - What direction are we flying?
3. Map preparation — Have students draw a map showing the desired flight path between two locations. Supply them with some elements to make the task doable: a part of the map they are to develop, a compass rose, and a point of departure ("You are here"). The students use the logbook to draw the airplane's path. They show the missing areas of the map, indicate distances between buildings, and estimate altitudes.

National Standards:
NCTM Mathematics Standards for Grades K–4
- STANDARD #1: Mathematics as problem solving
- STANDARD #4: Mathematical connections
- STANDARD #6: Number sense and numeration

Geography Standards for K–4
The World in Spatial Terms
- STANDARD #1: How to use maps and other geographic representations

Required Resources:
Flight simulation software such as Microsoft's *Flight Simulator*; a teacher-prepared worksheet for review.

◆ ◆

Title: Investigating Graveyard Data with Spreadsheets
Grade Level: 9–12
Source: Paul, J., and Kaiser. C. (1996). Do women live longer than men? Investigating graveyard data with computers. *Learning and Leading with Technology, 23*(8), 13–15.

Objectives/Purposes:
- Summarize information by creating a database and entering data into it.
- Draw conclusions from information summaries in databases.
- State and test hypotheses using database queries.

In this activity, students visit local graveyards, gather headstone data, enter them into a database, and answer questions about lifespan through database queries.

Procedures:
1. Collecting the data — Students work together in pairs, first dividing up the rows they will work on so that all will be covered and none duplicated. They use a data collection sheet to gather: surname, first name, date of death, age at death, and other details they think relevant (e. g., cause of death, if noted). Students will need to use math skills to calculate the age at death from the data on birth date and date of death provided on the headstone.
2. Inputting data — After all the data is collected, the class should be divided into three groups, and each group will enter the data in 2-hour sessions (other appropriate groupings and time frames

may be used). The database should be set up ahead of time and should mirror the data sheet.

3. Querying the database — Students scroll through the data to get a feel for what is covered and how it looks in summary form. They can sort data alphabetically by surname to see what families are represented. The teacher then asks students to form some questions to ask about the data and what it shows. Some questions that may be used are:
   - Who lives longer, women or men?
   - In which century did people live the longest (average age at death)?
   - What is the current average age of people when they die?
   Students then sort the data by date of death and by age to count occurrences in specific age or year categories. Students work in pairs to make tables and graphs to represent their findings. Once these graphs are completed, the whole class should hold a discussion on the findings.

National Standards:
NCTM Mathematics Standards for Grades 9–12
- STANDARD #1: Mathematics as problem solving
- STANDARD #3: Mathematics as reasoning
- STANDARD #10: Statistics
NSTA Science Standards for 9–12
- Science in Personal and Social Perspectives: Population growth
NCTE English/Language Arts
- STANDARD #7: Students conduct research on issues and interests by generating ideas and questions and by posing problems.
- STANDARD #8: Use a variety of technological and informational resources to gather and synthesize information and to create and communicate knowledge.

Required Resources:
A local graveyard to visit; database software.

◆ ◆

English/Language Arts

The Standards

The National Council of Teachers of English (NCTE), in conjunction with the International Reading Association (IRA), has issued a set of twelve standards for English/Language Arts education in grades K–12. The detailed descriptions of many of these standards include references to technology integration. The first standard deals with students reading a variety of print and non-print resources from many genres to learn about themselves and their world. The detailed description of this standard recognizes that technology-based texts are an important form of communication in today's society. Therefore, students need to learn to use and understand many resources, including films, illustrations, maps, CD-ROMs, and computer-based multimedia resources. This same rationale for the inclusion of various technologies is included in the detailed description of the second standard, which deals with students reading a variety of materials from various time periods to understand the human experience.

The effective use of various forms of communication is a part of standard number four. This standard focuses on the students' ability to adjust their use of language, including style, conventions, and vocabulary, for effective communication for a variety of purposes and for a variety of audiences. With the advance of telecommunications into homes and schools, students need to be able to communicate effectively in traditional formats as well as via e-mail, multimedia projects, and non-text based channels. These same criteria are a part of standard five, in which students are asked to use a number of strategies for writing and the writing process as they communicate with a variety of audiences for many different purposes.

The sixth standard requires that students apply their knowledge of language, genre, and media to create a variety of print and non-print texts. Students will use a variety of technologies to work on grammar, punctuation, composition, editing, illustration, and other communication skills.

The seventh standard asks students to use a variety of resources, including those that are technology-based, to research, analyze, and synthesize information. The eighth standard builds on the seventh, by asking students to use a number of technological resources to gather, synthesize, and communicate information. Both of these standards can incorporate a variety of technology tools, including CD-ROM encyclopedias, print media, interactive video, videotapes, e-mail, and the World Wide Web.

Standard number eleven encourages students to become knowledgeable, reflective, creative, and critical members of a literacy community. Communication within this community can take place through traditional formats or via networks, e-mail, or the World Wide Web.

Standard number twelve also focuses on students' communication to a community. In this standard, students are asked to use a variety of communication formats to accomplish their own purposes, including enjoyment, information exchange, and learning. These forms of communication may include technological approaches such as video and e-mail (Standards for the English/Language Arts, 1996).

Technology can also be integrated into these and the other standards through the use of word processing and other forms of technology-based communications.

Using Common Technology Tools in English/Language Arts Education

Word Processors. The word processor is the most common computer-based tool in the area of English/Language Arts. Any writing activity can be done using this type of program, including creative writing, research paper writing, and peer editing.

Students can also use the word processor and its editing features to practice their communications skills. For example, students can be assigned the task of drawing a simple picture (perhaps using defined geometric shapes). After they complete their drawing, each student should enter the directions for drawing their picture into a word processing program. After the instructions have been typed, spell checked, saved, and printed, the students should be divided into pairs. Each pair of students will exchange their directions and attempt to draw the picture by following the typed instructions. Once each pair of students has completed their drawings, each new drawing should be compared to the original. If the pictures do not match, the pair of students should review the directions, and make any appropriate changes. The revised directions can then be tested by having another student follow them to draw the picture. Once students have completed this procedure, a class discussion should occur to talk about the successful drawing and any problems that occurred. While discussing the problems, the teacher can talk about communication and organization skills as well as how to write for an audience; it's not enough for the writer to know what a text means, the reader must also be able to understand it.

Students involved in this lesson develop communication skills, an understanding of the importance of writing clearly for an audience, organizational skills, editing skills, and word processing skills. The word processor is valuable in this lesson because it allows students to save and to easily revise their work.

Internet. The Internet can be used in the English/language arts classroom to research topics for reports, to research about and communicate with authors, and to communicate with other students. Students can also use the Internet as a place to publish their work.

Publishing is an important part of the writing process, and students tend to do better work when they know it will be shared with an audience. Students can use the writing skills they develop in class to create a story in any number of formats that can be published on the World Wide Web. Students can use the writing process of prewriting, writing, and editing to learn about different genres of literature as well as to write for an audience, use correct grammar and spelling, and accomplish character and plot development. Once the students have finished their work, it can be submitted to a variety of sites on the Internet, including *Storybook Park* (http://www.planetzoom.com/storybookpark.html).

This site welcomes publications from students and authors regardless of length and genre. Stories, serials, and poems are welcome, and are divided into the following topics: Adventure/Fantasy; For Tots (this section includes bedtime stories); Mystery; Nature; People and Culture; and Real Life. The guidelines for submission include the need for parental permission if the author is under 18 years of age. Material that is submitted may include illustrations, must be appropriate in content, and must be designed for children from ages 2 to 12.

Although this site only accepts materials for preschool and elementary students, older students can use this site to develop their writing skills by creating stories for younger children. Younger students can write stories for their own age group, or other students who may access this site.

In addition to the writing activities described above, this site can also be used as a source of reading material.

Hypermedia. Hypermedia programs also play a role in the English/language arts classroom. Students can use these programs to create presentations on authors and to create "choose your own adventure" texts. Students (and teachers) may also create interactive texts using original works or traditional reading material.

For example, *HyperStudio* could be used to input a short story that will be read in class. Students could identify difficult or unfamiliar words and create hypermedia links that would allow the user to click on the identified word for a definition or explanation. Important plot points could be highlighted so that a student could choose the link to learn about that plot point and its relation to the rest of the story. Hints about foreshadowing and character development could also be highlighted in this manner. Having students create this kind of program requires them to learn a great deal about the piece of literature and the literary devices used in its creation. It also allows students to practice their skills in interpretation of literature and communication about literature, and with a specific audience.

The same kind of links could be applied to a piece of poetry. In addition, taped readings of the poem could be part of the program to allow the students to hear the rhyme and meter of the poem. Students can do the readings themselves to practice their skills with identifying meter and rhyme.

These student programs can be used for review, for authentic assessment, or for use by other classes or grade levels.

English/Language Arts Lesson Plans

❖ ❖

Title: Writing Through Webbing for Elementary Students
Grade Level: Primary
Source: Etchinson, C. (1995). A powerful web to weave—Developing writing skills for elementary students. *Learning and Leading with Technology, 23*(3), 14–15.

Objectives/Purposes:
• Write down and organize information on which to base written descriptions.
• Use a 5-step process to create written self-descriptions.
This lesson addresses the problem very young students have with beginning writing. They have a lot to say, but often it is difficult for them to get started. The author proposes a five-step writing curriculum:

Think ⟶ Draw ⟶ Tell ⟶ Write ⟶ Share

Through the following procedures, teachers introduced their students to this five-step process and encourage them to use it to start writing.

Procedures:
1. Preparation to write — This activity is used at the beginning of

the school year when students are excited about meeting new people. Each teacher takes a photo of the students in the class in order to insert it in their written documents. Students are encouraged to think about what they will write by describing themselves to the class in terms of their favorite food, sports, TV shows, and pets. The discussion may branch out to other areas such as vacations and future plans.

2. Planning through webbing — Students enter the information about themselves into a "webbing" template. Each student's picture is scanned into a pict. file and placed in the center of the student's web. A copy of the web should be printed out for each student. The chart serves to organize graphically students' ideas that they may draw on for their writing.

3. Writing activities — Using the information in the web, students begin composing a summary about themselves. Students choose the font and size and color of type for their document, and the teacher or parent assistant enters the information into a word processing file as the students dictate it. Students work with the teacher or assistant to correct spelling and prepare a final copy to print out and share with the whole class. The *ClarisWorks* Slideshow option can be used to present the final products on the screen.

National Standards:
NCTE English/Language Arts
- STANDARD #5: Students employ a wide range of strategies as they write and use different writing process elements appropriate to communicate with different audiences.

Required Resources:
ClarisWorks or other software with word processing, graphics, and "slideshow" options; optical scanner and scanning software to scan in photos.

❖ ❖

Title: Rhyming Time
Grade Level: K–4, students with learning disabilities
Source: Harrold, D., Strickland, B., Durr, G., DiResta, R. M., and Evans, M. (1991). Rhyming time. *The Florida Technology in Education Quarterly, 3*(2), 71–72.

Objectives/Purposes:
*   Hear rhyming words.
*   Read words that rhyme.
*   Create new nursery rhymes.

This lesson, designed for elementary students with varying exceptionalities, focuses on language development through the use of rhymes. Use of word processing with graphics helps provide a vehicle for creative expression and gives good visual feedback to students as they work.

Procedures:
1. Ask the students their favorite nursery rhymes. Have them say them if they can; if not, the teacher will say or read the rhyme. Identify rhyming words by use of word cards. Expand this activity over several days, if necessary, discussing the importance of rhymes; let students say words that rhyme aloud in class.
2. Tell the class they will be writing their own nursery rhymes. This can be either an individual activity or group activity. Use a word processing program to show the rhymes as they are made and a graphics program to create pictures to illustrate them.
3. Read rhymes written by class, using a large monitor or projection panel connected to the computer. Encourage students to create stories and other rhymes through language experience activities, stories, and sentence starters. Have them type their stories using a word processor appropriate for the age group.
4. This lesson could be expanded to include the development of rhyming cards using the computer and creating a publication of rhymes using word processing or desktop publishing software.

National Standards:
*   STANDARD #3: Students use a wide range of strategies to comprehend, interpret, evaluate, and appreciate texts.

Required Resources:
Word processing or desktop publishing software; graphics software.

❖ ❖

Title: Kids in the News
Grade Level: 5–8
Source: Bullock, D. (1993). Kid-to-kid news: A video language arts project. *The Computing Teacher, 20*(6), 27–28, 55.

Objectives/Purposes:
- Research and write news stories and commercials as components of a school news program.
- Videotape the news program and present it to the school.

This activity is proposed as a way to give kids motivational opportunities for reading, writing, speaking, and listening. Students create their own video news program and present it once a month to the school. The process of creating the news show consists of the following activities:

Procedures:
1. Research — Discuss with the students some possible news reports and commercials related to school activities. (Commercials can advertise school events or fund-raisers.) Make a list on the board of students' suggestions and ask for volunteers to research, write, and report on the topics. After the "news teams" prepare questions for their interviews, the teacher and class review and revise them. Students begin their research, interviewing school staff and students to obtain their information.
2. Writing — After the students gather all the information from their sources, they write their scripts. There is constant revising and editing until the final video is done. Groups help each other correct and edit their work. The teacher reviews the final scripts for accuracy and grammatical structure and news teams do final editing.
3. Rehearsing and taping — The teams decide who will present their stories and commercials and how they will be presented. A deadline for the final taping has been set in advance, and the students rehearse up until the deadline. The class as a whole decides the order for the newscast and two students are selected to "anchor" the program. Students who will not be presenting the newscast have other assignments such as announcing, operating the camera, and directing. Finally, the whole crew rehearses together and the videotape is completed.
4. Presenting the news — After taping is done, the class develops and word processes a list of questions that other students may answer as they watch the show. The newscast is scheduled and shown in other classrooms of the school. The presenters analyze

their own products, as well, deciding how they could do better next time.

National Standards:
NCTE English/Language Arts
* STANDARD #3: Students use a wide range of strategies to comprehend, interpret, evaluate, and appreciate texts.
* STANDARD #8: Students use a variety of technological and informational resources (e. g., libraries, networks, databases, and video) to gather and synthesize information and to create and communicate knowledge.

Required Resources:
Enough computers for the number of students in the group; word processing and graphics software; video camera with tripod; VCR and TV with a 26" screen; and a cart for transporting the TV and VCR.

❖❖❖❖❖❖❖❖❖❖❖❖❖❖❖❖❖❖❖❖❖❖❖❖❖

Title: Critics Corner via E-mail
Grade Level: 9–12
Source: Daniels, J., and Bryan, J. (1992). Critics corner. *The Florida Technology in Education Quarterly, 4*(2), 59–60.

Objectives/Purposes:
* Improve critical thinking and writing skills by doing a written evaluation of a piece of literature.

If students are still functioning several reading levels below normal by the time they are sophomores in high school, something unique and different is necessary to capture their interest and convince them to continue trying to improve their communication skills. This activity uses collaboration with other students on literary critiques via e-mail to provide that extra interest. Another way to increase motivation in conjunction with this activity is to have students write critiques on topics connected with special events (e. g., mystery stories or Gothic tales during October; love and romance during February; sports during various playoff seasons).

Procedures:
1. Preparation — Set up a mail distribution list of students who will receive the critiques. In this way, all students will receive each critique that is written and sent. Students may be either within the school or in various locations, depending on what the teacher is able to arrange. (The broader the audience, the more

motivating the students seem to find it.)

2. Assignment — Each student is assigned a short story written at the student's independent reading level. The teacher tells the students that they each will write a 1–2 paragraph critique of the story to be shared with others via e-mail. Encourage them to write about what they think of the story, e. g., how well they feel it was written and what emotions and thoughts it elicited in them.

3. Evaluation — Provide opportunities for students to study samples of other students writing and evaluate the standards for their own work. This technique helps in developing student portfolios. Students critique their own writing by finding guidelines in other students' writing. The teacher uses a printout to check students' work and, when the revisions are complete, adds the printout to the students' portfolios. The media specialist observes the choice of stories and includes this information for future additions to the library book collection. Upon completion of the short story assignment, students follow the same format for a book review and a movie review.

National Standards:
NCTE English/Language Arts
- STANDARD #6: Students apply knowledge of language structure, language conventions, media techniques, figurative language and genre to create, critique, and discuss print and nonprint texts.
- STANDARD #5: Students employ a wide range of strategies as they write and use different writing process elements appropriate to communicate with different audiences for a variety of purposes.
- STANDARD #8: Students use a variety of technological and informational resources (e. g., libraries, networks, databases, and video) to gather and synthesize information and to create and communicate knowledge.

Required Resources:
Computers set up with e-mail access; classroom or student e-mail accounts.

❖ ❖

❖ ❖

Title: A Project with Teeth
Grade Level: K–3, can be used with talent development students
Source: Boehm, D. (1997). I lost my tooth! *Learning and Leading with Technology, 24*(7), 17–19.

Objectives/Purposes:
- Create and analyze information in simple line and bar graphs.
- Use maps and globes to identify geographical locations.
- Write short messages to be used for e-mail.
- Identify cross-cultural themes in literature.
- Write paragraphs analyzing stories and legends.

Teachers use e-mail to connect their K-3 students with "keypals" around the world in order to exchange information on how many teeth the children lose during the year. This activity is used as a springboard for learning geography (locations of the keypals), literature and culture (tooth-fairy traditions and other stories from their region), art (creating pictures or murals illustrating tooth-fairy traditions), creative writing (e-mail messages to participants, poems and rhymes on teeth), and mathematics (graphing data on lost teeth).

Begin by preparing a bulletin board to stay in the classroom throughout the length of the project. Place on it a large happy face and 13 large "teeth" made out of paper, cardboard, or tag board. The first twelve teeth should each be labeled with a month of the year and the last should say, "I still have all of my teeth." Each time a student loses a tooth, write the name of the student on the "tooth" with the month in which it was lost. Find out from parents which students have lost teeth prior to the beginning of the project and label the appropriate months for them. Names of students who have lost no teeth are put on the "I still have all of my teeth" sign.

Do number 1 and some or all of the rest of the following activities.

Procedures:
1. The introductory e-mail message — With the students' input, write a letter describing the project. Include a time line (e.g., a semester or a school year); how you will communicate your results to each other (e.g., e-mail, snail-mail, graphs); and information you would like to have them send EACH MONTH (e.g., their location, number of teeth participating students have

lost, local traditions about lost teeth, items of information about their region).

2. A class story — After you have gathered stories from the other students, begin a class story on tooth traditions and legends. You can assign each student to write a part of the story and enter the text into a word processing file as students dictate their paragraphs to you.

3. Locating participants — Give each student a world map. As participants send their responses, have students mark and/or color the location on the map from where the message was sent. Also have globes and wall-maps around the room for students to examine as responses come in.

4. Tooth-fairy mural — Have students use art media or a graphics programs such as *Kid Pix* to create illustrations for the tooth-fairy stories and tooth traditions they have gathered. They can also add their own poems and rhymes to their mural.

5. E-mail letters — Show students how to create, send, receive, and print e-mail messages. Students may work individually or in small groups to prepare their messages.

6. Graphing lost tooth data — After you have at least three months of data on lost teeth, show students how to use a spreadsheet or graphing program to compile the data and prepare line or bar graphs. Each student or small group may choose a part of the data to graph, then compose a letter explaining the results to their keypals. As a cumulative or final whole-class activity, students may use a calculator to add up all the teeth data for each month from all the schools, then enter all the data into one common spreadsheet. Results may be shared among the participants through e-mail or file-sharing.

National Standards:
NCTM Mathematics Standards for Grades K–4
- STANDARD #2: Mathematics as communication
- STANDARD #4: Mathematical connections
- STANDARD #11: Statistics and probability

Geography Standards for K–4
- STANDARD #1: How to use maps and other geographic representations

NCTE English/Language Arts
- STANDARD #4: Students adjust their use of spoken, written, and visual language to communicate effectively with a wide variety of audiences and for different purposes.
- STANDARD #7: Students conduct research on issues and interests by generating ideas and questions and by posing

problems.

- STANDARD #8: Use a variety of technological and informational resources to gather and synthesize information and to create and communicate knowledge.
- STANDARD #9: Students develop an understanding of and respect for diversity in language use, patterns, and dialects across cultures, ethnic groups, geographic regions, and social roles.

Required Resources:
A computer connected to a large monitor or LCD panel and set up for Internet access; word processing, graphing (e.g., Tom Snyder Productions' *The Graph Club*), and graphics (e. g., Broderbund's *Kid Pix*) software; individual and wall-sized maps of the world and U. S.; globes; folders for each student.

❖ ❖

Title: Multimedia Descriptions of Native American Legends
Grade Level: 5–12
Source: Beekman, G. (1992). Recreating Native American legends with *HyperCard*. *The Computing Teacher, 19*(5), 31.

Objectives/Purposes:
- Research Native American legends for the local area.
- Develop a multimedia product to document and illustrate Native American legends.

Procedures:
1. Research — Identify materials which students can use to carry out their research on Native American legends. These might include books and articles, as well as websites and local museums. Have students form small groups to review the materials and choose one or more legends to work on.
2. Production — If students are not already familiar with it, introduce the features of the multimedia software. Show one or more sample products similar to what they will do. Let them design the artwork and graphics that will illustrate their descriptions.
3. Sharing — Have students share their products and give reports on their legends. Combine the products into a multimedia slide show for display to other classes or groups.

National Standards:
U. S. History Standards for Grades 5–12
- Eras 1–3 and 5

NCTE English/Language Arts Standards
- STANDARD #2: Students read a wide range of literature from many periods and many genres to build an understanding of the many dimensions of human experience.
- STANDARD #7: Students conduct research on issues and interests by generating ideas and questions and by posing problems.
- STANDARD #8: Students use a variety of technological and informational resources (e. g., libraries, networks, databases, and video) to gather and synthesize information and to create and communicate knowledge.

Required Resources:
Multimedia software such as *HyperCard* or *HyperStudio*; materials on Native American legends in the state or local area.

❖ ❖

Title: Technology Helps Save the Whales!
Grade Level: 5–8
Source: Edwards, J. (1993). Whales awareness project. *The Florida Technology in Education Quarterly, 5*(3), 100–101.

Objectives/Purposes:
The activities described here are designed to take a theme that is of high interest to children (whales), and use it as a vehicle to develop an interest in math, science, and research. Also, these activities provide a way for interest in ecology to be turned into action.

As a prerequisite, it is important that the students have a strong knowledge base concerning whales. After they have this knowledge base, the teacher should function primarily as a facilitator and allow the children to make as many of the production decisions as possible.

Procedures:
1. Introduction — Introduce the idea of a "whale awareness" week that could involve all grade levels and place emphasis on the need for people to know more about how ecological issues affect them. Have the class brainstorm possible activities to raise awareness. This is a very important phase. Be sure to provide opportunities for the class to generate ideas; it is crucial they feel

"ownership" of these ideas. However, the teacher should feel free to give suggestions. Some possible activities include:

- Word process and present a play centering around the plight of the whale.
- Present a Level 1 interactive videodisc lesson on whales to another class.
- Give students responsibility for ordering relevant materials (e.g., videos, software, videodiscs, CDs) from the county media center and inform the classroom teachers of their availability.
- Present facts, poems, or dramatizations about whales on morning announcements.
- Schedule a student production to be presented on closed circuit TV or show a relevant tape from the media center a few times during the week.
- Conduct a school-wide whale poetry or poster contest.
- Allow students to use a desktop publishing program to create an information bulletin presented in a newsletter format.
- Create a database on whales to donate to the media center. Fields may include: name, size, diet, and estimated population.

2. Set up committees — Help the class divide into committees that will focus on specific areas of the selected project. Possible committees include: media, publicity, education, entertainment, and art.

3. Committees choose projects — Groups need to select which project they would like to work on. Be flexible here; the process is what is really important. Teachers should require a written plan from the group that includes a detailed description of their project and what resources they will need.

4. Develop projects — Groups will now work on developing their projects. Allow ample time and provide direction. This is an important time for the teacher to be very active in monitoring the groups' progress. Many of the children will have a tendency to rush through and do a superficial job. Through probing, questioning, and guidance, the teacher can help assure quality.

5. Recognition — Provide opportunities for the work to be displayed and recognized by others in the school and local community.

National Standards:
NSTA Science Standards for Grades 5–8
- Science as inquiry
- Life science
- Science in personal and social perspectives

NCTE English/Language Arts
- STANDARD #7: Students conduct research on issues and interests by generating ideas and questions and by posing problems.
- STANDARD #8: Students use a variety of technological and informational resources to gather and synthesize information and to create and communicate knowledge.

Required Resources:
Resources include word processing software; desktop publishing software; video development resources; videodiscs with images of whales.

❖ ❖

Social Sciences

The Standards

The National Council for the Social Studies has developed ten standards for students in grades K–12. These standards present a number of opportunities for technology integration. For example, standard #3, People, Places and Environment, addresses the need for students at all grade levels to use various resources to gather, interpret, and manipulate information. Technology can be integrated into this standard through CD-ROM atlases, computer-generated charts and graphs, electronic databases, and photographs from a variety of sources, including satellites and the World Wide Web.

Linked to this standard is the first standard for each grade range, K–4, 5–8 and 9–12, proposed in the national Geography Standards. This geography standard focuses on the use of maps and other geographic representations as well as various tools and technologies to gather, interpret and present spatial information.

Technology can be integrated into other geography standards as well. Many of these standards expect students to be able to interpret and create maps, research information on climate, culture and other relevant topics, create graphs and charts, and communicate research findings. Programs such as *Cartopedia: The Ultimate World Reference Atlas*, published by Dorling Kindersley, can be used by students to examine and interpret many types of maps. Paint and drawing programs can be used to create maps. Electronic encyclopedias, the World Wide Web, and e-mail can be used to gather information on relevant topics. Spreadsheets and graphics programs allow students to create charts, graphs, and other visuals. Students can communicate their findings through these graphics programs as well as via word processing programs, web page authoring software, and multimedia presentation packages.

This general approach to technology integration is also a part of the standards for Economics issued by the National Council for Economic Education. These standards specifically mention technology as a part of Standard #15 for grades K–4, which expects them to complete a task such as a math worksheet by hand and then complete it using technology. Students are then asked to compare the accuracy and the time it took to complete the task by hand and with technology. Technology tools are also specifically mentioned in the general description for Standard #18. This standard expects students to use media reports to interpret information about current economic conditions. Although these standards are the only two that specifically mention technology as a tool, there are many ways that technology can be used to support the Economics standards. For example, when students are asked to research available products or to compare prices of products, they can use the Internet to visit online stores and catalogs. Students can also use spreadsheets to meet the requirements of various standards by calculating costs, profits and interest rates and the total cost of an item purchased with borrowed funds. Spreadsheets can also be used to help students create and maintain budgets. (Standard #10, for grades K–4, requires that students be able to plan a budget.) Technology can also be used to help students meet the requirements of standards dealing with currency rates (for example, Standard #7 for grades 5–8). They can access current exchange rates via the Internet and they can use spreadsheets to calculate what one would have to pay in American dollars for items from England, Canada, Italy, and other countries.

Economics students can also use the computer and related technologies to create presentation materials and information resources. Some of these materials include flowcharts, graphs, bar charts, and timelines.

Using common technology tools in social sciences education

Word Processors. Word processors are versatile tools that can facilitate writing in any subject area. In the social sciences, they can be used for the recording and reporting of data, communicating with public officials, and expressing opinions on current events.

Students can also use the word processor to create a class newspaper outlining the historic events and culture of a specific time period. For example, students who are studying the Civil War can create a newspaper from the day after the Battle of Bull Run. Students can be divided into two groups, one to create newspaper from a northern city and one to create a newspaper from a southern city. Assignments can then be divided among the students in each group. Some can do historical reporting on the battle, describing what happened on the battlefield and the results of the battle. These students may choose to include "interviews" with the general or other soldiers who had participated in the battle. They can use textbooks, biographies, or the World Wide Web to find relevant information for these interviews. Other students may be responsible for creating opinion pieces and editorials to include in the paper. These pieces might present opinions on the war, on the performance of the President, and feelings about secession and slavery. Students may also be asked to write articles about other events occurring at the same time, including world events and reviews of popular literature. The students can create their articles using a word processor. These articles would be assembled into a newspaper by the assigned editors and possibly shared with other classes studying the Civil War.

This activity allows students to examine both United States and world history of the 1860s. It provides them with the opportunity to synthesize information and to gain a better understanding of one of the major events in United States history.

Internet. The Internet provides students in the social science classroom with access to current events, maps, information on countries, and ways to communicate with people from other cultures.

Civics and Government classes can also benefit from the use of the Internet. Students in these classes can use the Internet to contact their local, state and national representatives. They can also access information on government programs, election issues, and speeches made by government officials.

One website that would be beneficial to a Civics or Government class, as well as a history class, is the White House site (http://www.whitehouse.gov). This site allows students to learn about the current President and Vice President, past Presidents and the White House. Students can also access presidential speeches, view photographs and White House documents, and access information on federal services such as medicare, financial aid and the patent office. Current events are also available via this site, with links to the "Briefing Room" which contains the day's news releases and current Federal statistics on a variety of topics, including economic and social statistics. Students can also access current happenings at the White House and the President's current programs. There is also a link to the White House for Kids for younger students. This website helps support the NCSS standard on Power, Authority, and Governance (standard #6).

Students may also use the Internet to work with all of the Geography standards. National Geographic's website has a link from its Kids section devoted to the application of these standards. The site is divided into six sections, with each one representing one of the main areas of the geography standards. Students can choose an area to study, and then further explore information related to the specific standards for each heading. For example, if a student chooses to explore the main area of The World in Spatial Terms, they may investigate standard #2 dealing with mental maps. In this section students can explore the differences in mental maps created by different people. The example shows a mental map of a kitchen from the perspective of a child and that of an adult. Corresponding text provides some information on the differences, and students may use this example as a springboard for a discussion of various mental maps. The address for the National Geographic website is http://www.nationalgeographic.com/resources/ngo/education/xpedition s/main.html

Hypermedia. Hypermedia allows social science students to present information using audio, video, illustrations, and text. Students can create programs highlighting a specific state or country. They can also outline the process used to make a bill into a law or create an interactive map of the world.

Students can use hypermedia to present their research on a specific topic in history such as the Civil Rights Movement of the 1960s. After researching information on the movement, students can create a text summary of their research. This summary can include links to information on famous people, and civil rights programs. Audio links can include excerpts Martin Luther King Jr.'s "I Have a Dream" speech and news reports from that time. Photos of marches, segregation signs, and other relevant images can be scanned into the program. Students can also include first-person recollections as text or audio. This activity can be used as a starting point for a discussion on the current state of civil rights in the United States as well as civil rights and issues of discrimination in other countries. This program can also be used as a reference tool for other social science classes.

Social Sciences Lesson Plans

❖ ❖

Title: *Kid Pix* in Multicultural Education
Grade Level: K–4
Source: Chan, B. (1993). *Kid Pix around the world: A multicultural activity book.* Reading, MA: Addison-Wesley Publishing Company.

Objectives/Purposes:
- Use Broderbund's *Kid Pix* to develop products (e.g., masks, collages) around cultural themes.

Since it was introduced several years ago, *Kid Pix* graphics software has become a popular resource in elementary classrooms. *Kid Pix* is now part of a package called *The Amazing Writing Machine*, which includes capabilities to combine graphics with writing activities. The Teacher Manual for this software is filled with ideas for using the package's drawing, painting, stamping, and text capabilities to support learning activities ranging from mathematics to language arts. Chan's book focuses on using *Kid Pix* in multicultural learning activities; a few of the ideas from this book are summarized here.

Procedures/Activities:

1. Picture Stories — The Inuit (whom many people commonly call Eskimos) at one time were a people largely dependent on fishing for their livelihood. Fishing was a common theme in their language and stories, which the Inuit liked to document by painting pictures on wooden objects. As students learn about the Inuit and other cultures who illustrated their histories in this way, they can use *Kid Pix* rubber stamps to create their own stories or tell about their own histories or those of their families. The teacher can begin by telling or reading an Inuit adventure and use *Kid Pix* to illustrate it as it unfolds.

2. Illustrated Songs — Many cultures love songs and singing. Early settlers from Spain brought their canciones (Spanish for songs) with them to North and Central America. Students can use the Spanish language features of *Kid Pix* to write and illustrate songs in Spanish that will give them practice in using the language. They can write both the Spanish version and the English translation on the screen, then illustrate it with stamps or other draw features.

3. Creating Totem Poles — Native Americans of the Pacific Northwest carved totem poles to record the histories of their tribes and families. Students can use *Kid Pix* to create their own totem poles which tell about themselves and their families.

4. Designing a Good-bye Cloth — Long ago, the people of Ghana would create a special cloth with designs and symbols from their culture as a gift for someone who left for another village. The Ghanians called the fabric "Adrinka" (goodbye) cloth after the dye used to produce the designs. Students can create unique designs for their own "goodbye cloths." They can produce symbols that stand for events or emotions and repeat the design over the screen as they wish. This design can be printed out several times and pasted or taped together to form a wall hanging or wrapping paper.

5. Creating Masks — Many cultures create masks to use in rituals, to protect themselves against evil spirits or gods, or to present plays or tell stories. Children in the United States use masks to observe events such as Halloween. Students can use *Kid Pix* features to design their own masks for use in plays or dramatizations. When the paper design is finished, it can be printed out and made into a three-dimensional mask.

6. Creating Collages — Paper collage is an activity common to many cultures. People use collages as artistic products or to tell about themselves. Each image of the collage tells something about their

culture or their history. Collages done with small pieces of stone or shells are another kind of collage called a mosaic. Students can use *Kid Pix* to create their own paper collages or mosaics to tell about themselves and/or their families. In addition to *Kid Pix* draw and stamp features, students can add scanned-in photos or other pictures to their *Kid Pix* collage.

National Standards:
HISTORY Standards for Grades K–4
- Topic 4—The History of Peoples of Many Cultures Around the World

Required Resources:
Broderbund's *Kid Pix* (now part of *The Amazing Writing Machine*)

◆ ❖ ❖ ❖ ❖ ◆ ❖ ❖ ❖ ❖ ❖ ❖ ❖ ❖ ❖ ❖ ❖ ❖ ❖ ❖ ❖ ❖ ❖ ❖ ❖ ◆

Title: Teaching the Bill of Rights with Graphics
Grade Level: 5–8
Source: Reissman, R. (1994). Rights conflict computer scenarios— Storyboarding and "righting" our responsibilities. *The Computing Teacher, 22*(2), 34–35.

Objectives/Purposes:
- Research the history, meaning, and implications of each of several Bills of Rights.
- Analyze and interpret concepts behind a Bill of Rights.
- Demonstrate an understanding of the Bill of Rights by developing a Bill of Rights for a given group or purpose.

This lesson addresses the problem many 10- to 11-year old students have with understanding the meaning and implications of the Bill of Rights and how it relates to their own school behavior codes. The students use a combination of drawing and word processing software to make these dry words come to life and communicate the rights and responsibilities they stand for.

Procedures:
1. Getting started — The teacher divides the class into groups of three students each. They use the word processor to take notes as they review the Bill of Rights and select what they feel are the most important three rights. Members of each of the groups share their findings with their group members. They arrive at a common set of top three choices for their group and enter them into the file along with the reasons they consider them so

important. The teams present their findings on a large monitor so the whole class can see them. They put a bullet beside those that were chosen by more than one group. The bullets indicate where there is agreement on key guarantees of the Bill of Rights. As a class, they decide on the top three. (The teachers referenced in the source for this lesson found that students normally chose Article 1 (freedom of speech, religion, press, and assembly) as the first choice; Article 5 (rights of the accused) as the second choice; and Article 6 (due process) as the third choice.)

2. Illustrating the rights — The teacher gives each group a storyboard and asks them to develop a scenario where exercising one of these rights might lead to conflict. They may either draw the scene using drawing software, or write about it with the word processor. They are to leave the scenarios open-ended, without recommending a resolution. The groups present their scenarios to the whole class, and students suggest ways of addressing the conflicts. One student acts as class recorder, using the word processor to note the rights scenarios and the possible solutions. For example:

Exercising Our Rights Scenarios	Potential Solutions
Article 1: Using bias-filled epithets on the playground.	Discuss what the epithets mean. Learn about each other's cultures and values.

After all scenarios have been discussed, have the teams discuss some ways implementing their solution strategies could help ensure group rights. Bring out the concept that these rights also imply responsibilities, and that the exercise of individual rights sometimes has to be limited in order to ensure group rights (e.g., if exercising freedom of speech incites people to riot, it must be limited to ensure the safety of everyone).

3. Follow-up activities — Students may do some or all of the following activities:

    •   Have teams of students develop their own Bill of Rights along with a Bill of Responsibilities that would help safeguard the rights. Have them present the bills to the class and ask for their ratification. If the class agrees to ratify them, let the students make up a parchment copy in calligraphy and post it on a bulletin board.

    •   Ask students to collect as many Bills of Rights as they can

find from local and community sources (e.g., Dry Cleaner's Bill of Rights, Patient's Bill of Rights). Have them prepare a Bill of Responsibilities for each of these rights.
- Ask students to compare our nation's Bill of Rights with that of the United Nations. Have them prepare a Bill of Responsibilities for each of these rights.
- Have students identify one or more special interest groups that need a Bill of Rights and a Bill of Responsibilities (e.g., animals, AIDS victims, or even alien life forms). Get the students to invite real or imaginary representatives from these groups to help draft the bills. Also invite advocates of the opposite rights (e.g., businesses that oppose animal rights groups) to have them share their opinions. Ask students to listen to both sides and write a persuasive essay on their views of these rights.

National Standards:
Civics and Government Standards for Grades 5–8
- What are civic life, politics, and government?
U. S. History Standards for Grades 5–12
- Era 3: Revolution and the New Nation

Required Resources:
Drawing and word processing software.

❖ ❖

Title: Virtual Field Trips
Grade Level: 9–12
Source: Goldsworthy, R. (1997). Real-world field trips. *Learning and Leading with Technology, 24*(7), 26–28.

Objectives/Purposes:
- Organize and plan a trip to a city.
- Use map skills to determine itineraries in a city.
- Use the World Wide Web to obtain trip-planning information.
- Plan and write documents to summarize information about a trip.
Even though students may not be able to take educational trips to far-off places, they can take "virtual field trips" by visiting Internet websites. Designing and carrying out such field trips is a complex learning experience that involves problem solving and content-area skills ranging from map reading to research. (The field trip described in this article was to Washington, D. C., but it could be used as a

model for "trips" to any other desired destination on the World Wide Web.)

After the initial decision on a location is made, in this case Washington, D.C., the "trip" has the following three components:

Procedures:
1. Research — Students have to determine what there is to visit in Washington, D. C., and what information is available on that location. They begin by using the Thomas web page (URL: http://thomas.loc.gov/) to locate fax numbers and other contact information for their senators and representatives. Students word process and fax letters to their representatives and to the President requesting information about Washington, D. C. Within 2 to 3 weeks, the class should receive a great deal of information from these contacts addressed to each student who had requested it. Students can also use the following web resources:
   - Search engines such as *Yahoo!* help them locate sites such as the home page for the Washington, D. C. Metropolitan Area Transit Authority, which has fares, stations, and maps for the Metro. They can also find a variety of other websites for famous Washington, D. C. locations such as the Smithsonian Institute.
   - Programs such as *MapQuest* and *TripQuest* help them obtain maps and find the shortest distance between cities.
2. Administration — Students use software office tools to handle clerical tasks associated with the trip. They can use spreadsheets to create a trip budget, word processing to write memos and permission slips, and paint/draw software to create a trip t-shirt. They should create two databases: one of names and contact information for places such as hotels, restaurants, and tourist attractions to help them decide where they want to visit during their trip; and one with parent, student, and chaperone names and addresses to keep track of planning tasks such as payments.
3. Reporting — Guidebooks, itineraries, and learning logs should be created to record places students will visit and what they would change for a next trip, and to share their experiences with others.

National Standards:
Geography Standards for 9–12
The World in Spatial Terms
- STANDARD #1: Use maps and other geographic representations, tools, and technologies to acquire, process, and report information from a spatial perspective.

Required Resources:
Computers with an Internet connection; database and spreadsheet software; *MapQuest* and *TripQuest* software.

❖ ❖

Interdisciplinary Lessons Involving Social Sciences

❖ ❖

Title: State History Bites on the Morning News
Grade Level: 2–4
Source: Holifield, D. (1992). A graphic history of Florida. *The Florida Technology in Education Quarterly, 4*(2), 82–83.

Objectives/Purposes:
• Research and write about a state history topic.
• Work cooperatively in groups to develop a video product about state history.
This activity is designed to keep student interest high while developing skills in research, social studies, and communication. Students use an electronic encyclopedia to research a topic in state history, then plan and develop videos designed to be shown on the school's closed circuit television "morning news program." (This activity is especially motivational if the state has a "history month" during which local news broadcasts feature highlights from the state's colorful past.)

Procedures:
1. Preparation and training — Divide students into cooperative learning groups to research a topic about the state and plan a script for video sequences. Stress that this is a cooperative activity and that each student should contribute to the final product. Students select or are assigned the roles of group leader, researcher, reporter, and artist. Allow the students to discuss their tasks and select a research topic which can include but is not limited to the following topics: area, location, climate, notable people, industry, interesting sites, unique plants or wildlife, natural resources, exploration, and expansion.
2. Student research — Begin by showing the groups how to use an electronic encyclopedia to locate information about their topic and how to gather appropriate pictures from the encyclopedia entries

and elsewhere. Students locate a list of possible articles to read and gather information and pictures from the articles.

3. Scripting a sequence — The students decide on the most important information to be included in the video report. After the basic decisions are made, they must organize the facts and write a script for a video sequence. They use a word processing program to write the script and a graphics program to produce visual props needed for the production.

4. Filming — The cooperative teams should assist each other with the staging and filming of each video segment. After the sequences are completed, they are shown as "History Briefs" in the school's morning broadcasts.

National Standards:
History Standards for Grades K–4
- Topic 2: The history of students' own state and region

NCTE English/Language Arts
- STANDARD #6: Students use a variety of technological and informational resources to gather and synthesize information and to create and communicate knowledge.

Required Resources:
An electronic encyclopedia (e.g., *Compton's Multimedia Encyclopedia*); video production equipment; word processing and graphics software.

❖ ❖

Title: A Multimedia Biome Project
Grade Level: 2–8; appropriate for Title I and at-risk students
Source: Bennett, N., and Diener, K. (1997). Habits of mind. *Learning and Leading with Technology, 24*(6), 18–21.

Objectives/Purposes:
- Develop "habits of mind" such as perseverance, cooperation, responsibility, and willingness to complete tasks.
- Create spreadsheets and graphs of data, such as rainfall.
- Identify the geographic location of various biomes.
- Identify the physical characteristics of various biomes.
- Research and report on information related to various biomes.
- Develop and present multimedia presentations on biomes.

This activity is designed to be an alternative to those that Title I students usually do with technology. In many schools, students who are having academic problems are placed in Title I programs which emphasize remedial basic skill instruction. Computers are used primarily for tutorial and drill activities to develop these skills. This project focuses instead on using multimedia development projects to foster what the authors call "habits of mind," such as perseverance, problem solving, and cooperation. The rationale is that students will be better able to learn any content area skills if they develop these mental capabilities. There is also an emphasis on developing communications skills and growth in writing ability.

Although this lesson is designed for Title I students, it can be used with any group of students.

Procedures:
1. Students are divided into cooperative groups of 2 to 3. Students are introduced to the topic of biomes and asked to select a biome they wish to study.
2. Each group of students formulates questions about their biome to be answered through research. They can look for information on its characteristics, its location on earth, its climate, and threats to its ecosystem.
3. To keep students on track and focused, they are asked to write down what they will work on each day; also, each student should keep a checklist of tasks to be begun, completed, or revised.
4. For their multimedia products, students should do the following:
   - Word process their biome reports and paste the text into fields on their cards in the multimedia program.
   - Choose photos from a Photo CD to make backgrounds for their cards.
   - Use *Kid Pix* to illustrate their reports.
   - Create maps showing the location of their biomes.
   - Create spreadsheets and graphs of data.
   - Write about and include pictures of animals in their biomes.
   - Draw pictures and use clip art and graphics programs to illustrate food chains.
   - Use a QuickTake camera to take pictures of themselves for Authors cards.
5. They can present their final multimedia stacks at a local city multimedia fair, at an evening presentation for parents, or to other classes in their school.
6. To assess student progress in this unit, teachers can use a chart to track writing skills and interview students on film to assess communication skills. As an exercise in metacognition, students can be asked to evaluate their own growth in "habits of mind."

National Standards:
NSTA Science Standards for Grades K–4
- Science as Inquiry — Employ simple equipment and tools to gather data and extend the senses. Communicate investigations and explanations.

NSTA Science Standards for Grades 5–8
- Science as Inquiry — Use appropriate tools and techniques to gather, analyze, and interpret data.
- Life Science — Populations and ecosystems.

NCTM Mathematics Standards for Grades K–4 and 5–8
- STANDARD #2: Mathematics as communication
- STANDARD #4: Mathematical connections

Geography Standards Grades K–4 and 5–8
The World in Spatial Terms
- STANDARD #1: How to use maps and other geographic representations, tools, and technologies.
- Places and Regions
- STANDARD #4: The physical and human characteristics of places.

Required Resources:
QuickTake camera; photos from a Photo CD (optional); clip art and a graphics program such as *Kid Pix;* a word processing program; and a multimedia program such as *HyperStudio.*

❖ ❖

Title: A KidsMall Project
Grade Level: 5–8
Source: Smith, P. (1996). KidsMall USA. *Learning and Leading with Technology, 23*(6), 65–67.
and
Smith, P. (1996). KidsMall USA. *Learning and Leading with Technology, 23*(7), 40–44.

Objectives/Purposes:
- Work cooperatively to develop a plan and carry it out.
- Plan, create, and operate a (simulated) small business.
- Use a spreadsheet to organize data on monetary transactions.

The KidsMall USA project was designed to give students an opportunity to use computer applications (e.g., spreadsheets, databases) in real-world problem solving. With this program students create their own small businesses at school and use computer tools to try to make the businesses profitable. Each student creates a business in which s/he is interested and the businesses are brought together to form a KidsMall. Activities involved in this project include:

Procedures:
1. Start-up activities — Students form teams of 2 to 3 members who are "business partners." The teacher enters their names and the names of their businesses into a database. Also, the teacher shows a videotape of what other students have done in the past (if available), which gives them ideas on what they might do. Each of the student groups receives a teacher-made project guidebook which contains directions and instruction sheets on how to use computer resources to design various materials for the business. These materials include:
   - Storefront design and floor plan for the store.
   - Interior decorating for the store.
   - Employee portfolio.
   - Model building of storefront.
   - Inventory management and store receipts.
   - Public relations plan and sample ads and billboards.
   - Opening day procedures.
   - Evaluation criteria and procedures and student follow-up report format.
   - Descriptions of the store's products.
2. Managing the projects — Students are allowed three days to complete each of the activities from step 1. A computer station is set up with the software required to complete each activity, and teams move from station to station every three days. They complete each activity sheet and turn them in to be graded according to criteria the teacher has set. The teacher goes from station to station monitoring and assisting the work. Teachers may also perform more technical functions such as taking slide "commercials" and developing a video.
3. Running the stores — On Opening Day, the students open their stores for business. Each store gets a checkbook and 50 receipts to record individual purchases. The store owners are also the customers, and they go to each others stores using the checks to "buy" things. For each purchase, they write a check and the store owners staple the check to the receipt.
4. Wrap-up and evaluating the work — After the buying and selling are finished, each store completes a spreadsheet to record the transactions. Students record the earnings, balance the checkbooks, and fill out the self-evaluations.

National Standards:
NCTM Mathematics Standards for Grades 5–8
- STANDARD #1: Mathematics as problem solving
- STANDARD #4: Mathematical connections

Economics Content Standards
- STANDARD #7: Markets exist when buyers and sellers interact.
- STANDARD #11: Money makes it easier to trade, borrow, save, invest, and compare the value of goods and services.

Required Resources:
Spreadsheet, database, and graphics (e.g., *Kid Pix*) software; teacher-created project guidebook with directions for each activity; cardboard to make storefronts.

❖ ❖

Title: Buy Low/Sell High: A Study of the Stock Market
Grade Level: 9–12
Source: Based on a lesson from *Productivity in the Classroom*. 1997. Microsoft Corporation. For a detailed copy of this lesson, visit this website:
http://www.microsoft.com/education/k12/resource/lessons.htm

Objectives/Purposes:
- Simulate a stock market investment and track the results over time.
- Calculate profit or loss for a given investment.

This lesson will teach students how to invest in corporate stocks by creating investment "portfolios." They will develop worksheets that track their portfolio's performance over a specified time period and report the results to the class.

Procedures:
1. Introduce the project — Introduce students to the stock market summarizing its role in U. S. economic history (e.g., the great crash of 1929). Define terms that students are likely to encounter in their research such as *portfolio, dividend,* and *price/earnings ratio* (i. e., stock price divided by stock earnings per share.) Have students bring in the business section of newspapers that publish stock market information and explain to them how to read a stock quote. Have each student choose ten companies whose stock they might want to purchase. Explain that everyone in the class will start with $1,500 as seed money to purchase stocks at the current market value and that they will track their portfolio's

performance over a period of time from six weeks to three months. Finally, discuss with students the effectiveness of line charts in presenting their results.

2. Research the market — Students use *Microsoft Encarta* and the Internet to choose ten possible companies in which they might invest. They access each company's Web site in order to gather as much background information as possible about each company, including:
   - Type of company
   - Number of years in business
   - Summary of what the company does
   - Last year's profits
   - This year's profits (thus far)

   Now they review the information gathered and decide on five companies in which to invest. They find out the current selling price per share for each company's stock and decide how many shares of stock they want to buy in each company, keeping in mind that they have only $1,500 to invest. *Encarta* includes several helpful articles about the stock market. Use the encyclopedia's Find command to search for keywords such as "Stocks and Bonds," "Finance," and "Stock Exchange."

   Also, have students visit the websites called "Investing for Kids" or "StockMaster," the stock market sites referenced in the Web Links section of *Encarta*. Or, they can access a wealth of business news and financial information to track the performance of selected stocks by visiting the website of "Microsoft Investor." The addresses for these websites are:
   - Investing for Kids (http://tqd.advanced.org/3096)
   - StockMaster (http://www.stockmaster.com)
   - Microsoft Investor (http://www.investor.msn.com)

3. Create a spreadsheet — In *Microsoft Excel*, create a worksheet for each of the five companies in their investment portfolio. For each company's worksheet, they will input (a) some basic information about the company, such as the company Symbol (the unique symbol assigned to a NASDAQ security) and the name of the particular Stock Exchange that lists the stock; (b) an Initial Investment section; and (c) a Daily Record section.

4. Invest in the companies — They create the Initial Investment and enter it in the investment section of their worksheet. Each day they enter information on their selected stocks in the Daily Record section of the worksheet.

5. Tracking stocks — At the end of the stock performance period, they use the Chart Wizard in *Microsoft Excel* to create a line chart showing "profit or loss" for each stock they've invested in.

6. Reporting results — Students summarize their stock market experience in a printed report using Word and incorporate worksheets and charts copied from *Microsoft Excel*. Or they can create a slide presentation using *Microsoft PowerPoint*. The presentation should summarize the company's stock performance and any trends that are apparent.
7. Extension activities: (a) Have students consider trading their stock (buying or selling shares) during the specified time period; (b) Have students create a Summary worksheet of their investments. Columns should contain cells that reference initial investments, total shares owned, current price/share, and profit/loss figures for every company in the portfolio.

National Standards:
NCTM Mathematics Standards for Grades 9–12
- STANDARD #2: Mathematics as problem solving
- STANDARD #4: Mathematical connections
National Content Standards for Economics
- STANDARD #8: Institutions evolve in market economies to help individuals and groups accomplish their purposes.

Required Resources:
Computers set up for Internet use; *Microsoft Encarta*; *Microsoft PowerPoint,* or other presentation software; word processing software; and spreadsheet software.

❖ ❖

Science

The Standards

The National Science Education Standards for K–12 students reflect the use of technology in the classroom. For all three grade groupings, K–4, 5–8, and 9–12, technology appears in the "Science as Inquiry" standard. In grades K–4, students are asked to use simple equipment and tools to gather their data. These tools can include computers and calculators to be used for measuring and recording data. For grades 5–8, the suggestion is to include the use of spreadsheets and creation of computer graphics in science education. These students are also asked to use appropriate tools and methods to gather, analyze, and interpret data. The tools that may be used in these processes should include computer software designed for scientific inquiry and data analysis. Students in grades 9–12 are also required to use computers to meet the standard of scientific inquiry. The standard states that these students can use the computers for collecting, analyzing, and presenting data.

Technology may also be used to help students in grades K–4 to meet content standard G: understanding science as a human endeavor. In this standard it is suggested that teachers use various forms of technology, including films and videos to present examples of people who have made contributions to science.

Students in grades 5–8 can meet part of the Life Science standard (content standard C) by using computers to help quantify data and using light microscopes to view cells and other microorganisms.

Technology may also be of value in helping students to meet the other content standards. The Internet can be used as a research and communication tool. Students can present research findings and information using such presentation packages as Microsoft's *PowerPoint*. Spreadsheets and databases are wonderful tools for recording and analyzing data. Students can also use drill and practice, tutorial, and game software to learn basic science information, including the steps in cell division and the types of volcanoes. Simulations would allow students to explore science concepts, including chemical reactions and genetics, in a safe environment that can be revisited as many times as necessary.

Using Common Technology Tools in Science Education

Word Processors. Students in science classes have a need to communicate the results of their experiments and investigations. The word processor is a perfect tool for this endeavor. In addition to reports about famous scientists or research on the impact of new and old scientific discoveries on society, students can create lab reports and scientific newsletters.

For example, students could learn about scientific inquiry and scientific reports by studying various science journals that report on the results of experiments. After examining these journals to identify procedures and methods for presenting results, the class identifies what experiment(s) they would like to conduct for publication in a school science journal.

One such experiment might involve students generating hypotheses about the rate at which a piece of hard candy dissolves. They could generate ideas about what would make the candy dissolve faster (place it in boiling water; move it around in one's mouth) or slower (don't move it around in one's mouth; try to dissolve it in water that already has sugar dissolved in it). They may even explore if different flavors or shapes of candy dissolve at different rates.

Once the students have generated the hypotheses, they would carry out experiments to test them. As they are completing the experiments, students can use the word processor to record their procedures and findings.

Students then use these drafts to compose their final research articles. They must make sure to include the procedures used in their experiments, any specific materials used, and the results of their study. These findings must be communicated in a manner that will be understandable to their audience.

The teacher or student editor combines these articles into a scientific journal that may include experiments from other classes. The finished product can be donated to the library for use by other students.

Internet. The Internet provides science students with access to current research, science fair projects, and even the opportunity to talk with scientists. The Internet can also be used as a tool in dissection.

As concerns for students' safety during dissection grows, virtual dissections are becoming an appropriate alternative. Students can use the Internet to access the Exploratorium Museum's website (http://www.exploratorium.edu/learning_studio/cow_eye/index.html) to complete a dissection of a cow's eye. At this site, students can learn how to dissect the eye, complete an interactive tutorial about eyes, access information about cow eyes and human eyes, and actually complete the dissection. This virtual dissection site allows students to repeat the dissection as many times as necessary. This helps to eliminate concerns about making an error during the dissection and destroying the cow's eye. Students can also use this website to link to sites that display pictures of a dissected cow's eye; these links can be used for reference before the dissection or for review afterward. A real dissection could follow an Internet practice session, or the Internet could be used to provide the entire experience.

Hypermedia. Students in science class can use hypermedia programs to create tutorial stacks on cell division, the life cycle of a plant, the types of rocks, and famous scientists.

This type of program could also be used to help students explore the solar system. As a collaborative project, students are divided into two groups with each group assigned one of the planets. Students then decide on the information to research for each planet. Some suggestions include: size, composition, year first discovered, findings from NASA probes that have visited the planet, and myths or stories about the planet. Once the class has determined the topics to research, a template for a stack in *HyperStudio* or some other hypermedia program highlighting these points would be designed.

Each group of students would then compile information about their planet and put it into a copy of the template. Students could use textbooks, magazines and newspapers, scientific journals, and the World Wide Web to find information and photographs on their planet. If time permits, the students could use the word processor to write letters to NASA requesting specific information.

Students can incorporate text and illustrations and may even want to include audio clips from Holst's symphony, *The Planets*, in their final stacks.

When all of the information is entered, appropriate links among stacks and among planets are identified and created. Students could then use this program as a review for a test, or as part of their science portfolio for the school year.

Science Lesson Plans

❖ ❖

Title: A Dinosaur Project
Grade Level: K–4
Source: Etchinson, C. (1995). Dinosaurs, computers, and integrating the elementary curriculum. *The Computing Teacher, 22*(5), 21–22.

Objectives/Purposes:
• Do research to locate information about specific dinosaurs.

- Create and display a multimedia slide show showing research findings about dinosaurs.

In this elementary-level project, a graphics program plays an integral role in helping display the students work in their unit about dinosaurs. The students begin by choosing a partner and deciding on a dinosaur they would like to research. They should have already had the opportunity to work with *Kid Pix* so they have enough experience with it to make a "dinosaur movie" of all the students' work using the slide show feature. The object of the activity is to learn one fact about their dinosaur, record a reading of the fact, and show a picture, that they create, of their dinosaur.

Procedures:
- Pairs of students are assigned to work together; the teacher should help them decide which dinosaur each pair will work on. The classroom teacher and Technology Resource Teacher (or other resource person, if available) should create a package of materials so that everyone will have the directions and resources they need to complete their work independently. Each pair should make one slide for the show with information about their dinosaur. The pairs should work together to decide how their slide will look and sketch it on paper. A committee of students can review each plan for the slide to make sure the facts are accurate and that all words are spelled correctly.
- If the classroom has only one computer, a practice schedule could be set so each pair of can practice with the *Kid Pix* tools to make the slide look the way they want. Then the students could do the actual work on designing the slides.
- Once all of the slides have been created, the students, as a class, vote on the transitions between slides they will use and design a beginning and ending slide.

National Standards:
NSTA Science Standards for Grades K–4
- Science as inquiry: Communicate investigations and explanations.

Required Resources:
Graphics software with slide show capability (e.g., *Kid Pix*).

❖ ❖

Title: A Database Project with Rocks
Grade Level: 5–8
Source: Hartson, T. (1993). Rocks, minerals, databases, and simulations. *The Computing Teacher, 21*(1), 48–50.

Objectives/Purposes:
- Identify minerals using tests for hardness, luster, cleavage, magnetic attraction, streak, and color.
- Develop a database of information on rock characteristics.
- Answer questions about rocks from database searches.

A unit of study on rocks can form the basis for learning science inquiry skills. A database on rocks helps organize the information to support several kinds of problem-solving activities.

Procedures:
1. Getting started — The National Geographic filmstrip *Rocks and Minerals* could be used to supply background information on the unit and to stimulate students' natural interest in rocks and minerals. However, any media that provide a good visual review could be used. After this introduction, the teacher introduces the three main types of rocks and the rock formation cycle. The students begin to collect rock samples to sort, observe, and classify. Using a mineral collection and testing apparatus, students test their mineral samples and identify them according to their findings. They test for streak, scratch, hardness, cleavage, magnetism, and luster. Also, they observe color and crystal formations. Pictures from books and laserdisc are used to supplement their study.
2. Research and database development — Students each select one mineral to research and gather information on. They enter the information they find into a database. The teacher and student then develop questions and use the database to answer them. Typical questions are:
     - Which crystal structures are the most common?
     - What makes certain minerals valuable?
     - What are the most valuable minerals used for?
     - Which minerals occur most often in (your location)?

A printed set of questions can be used later as a consolidating exercise.

National Standards:
NSTA Science Standards for Grades K–4 and 5–8
- Science as inquiry
- Earth and space science

Required Resources:
Text, film, and videodisc resources on rocks; a mineral collection and testing apparatus; database software.

◆ ◆

Title: Designing a Solar House
Grade Level: 9–12
Source: Guthrie, J., and Crane, B. (1992). Online retrieval adds realism to science projects. *The Computing Teacher, 19*(5), 32–33.

Objectives/Purposes:
- Do research to establish the requirements for a solar house.
- Design and test a physical model of a solar house.
- Use multimedia to make a presentation about solar houses.

A good example of a hands-on science project is having students design and test their own solar house. They can research the requirements for solar houses using online sources, test their designs with probeware, and make a presentation on solar houses with videodisc resources and multimedia software.

Procedures:
1. Introduce the project — Begin by showing students some examples of solar houses and discussing their advantages and disadvantages. Challenge them to research and design a model of a functional solar house, and make a presentation of their findings in a multimedia format.
2. Do the research — Show students websites, videodiscs, and other resources they can use to gather information on the requirements of solar houses. Have them form small groups to do the research and design models of their houses. Tell students they can use only cardboard, paint, tape, and insulation materials for their models.
3. Design the products — When students have completed their research and are ready to build their models, supply the building materials they need. Work with the groups to make the models. Demonstrate how to use the probeware to test the house. Then calibrate the probes, record the house temperature, use light to heat the house for 10 minutes, record the temperature, let the house cool for 10 minutes, and record the temperature again. Have groups compare and discuss their findings.
4. Develop a presentation — Show students how to develop a multimedia product that can display videodisc frames. They also may want to scan in and use pictures and diagrams from book and Internet resources they used in their research. Ask students

to develop and make presentations that document the kinds of features that they built into their models, why they achieved the results they did, and how their models could be improved. Share these presentations with the class and other groups.

National Standards:
NSTA Science Standards for Grades 5–8 and 9–12
- Physical science
- Science as inquiry
- Science and technology

Required Resources:
Websites, videodiscs, and other sources of information on solar houses; probeware to gather temperature data (e.g., Broderbund's *Science Toolkit*); cardboard, paint, tape, and insulation materials for building a house model; multimedia software.

❖ ❖

Title: Traits 'R Us: A Genetics Activity
Grade Level: 9–12
Source: Based on a lesson from *Productivity in the Classroom.* 1997. Microsoft Corporation. For a detailed copy of this lesson, visit this Microsoft website:
http://www.microsoft.com/education/k12/resource/lessons.htm

Objectives/Purposes:
- Create a database of information on genetic characteristics.
- Analyze a summary of genetic information to determine trends in characteristics.

In this supplement to their study of genetics, students learn more about heredity by collecting and analyzing information about their own and their classmates' characteristics (such as hair color and height) and traits (such as ability to roll tongue or raise one eyebrow). As the activity progresses, students will be amazed to discover the genetic diversity within their own classroom.

Procedures:
1. Introduce the project — Ask the class: How many of you can roll your tongues? Raise one eyebrow? Take a quick tally. Ask: Why do some people have these traits while others do not? Guide students toward understanding that these traits are hereditary, passed along the same way that hair and eye color are. Note that other hereditary traits include left- and right-handedness and the

ability to whistle. Tell students that they will be creating a database of genetic characteristics and traits in their own classroom. Have them brainstorm the fields for the database. Then divide your class into teams. Teams will work separately on the first step and combine forces for the remaining steps.

2. Create the data form — The students open the empty database and enter the fields they created earlier as a class. Each group creates a format to display the data. Each team presents its finished form on the overhead viewer. The class votes on a favorite, and saves it as the Class Form.

3. Enter the data — Each team of students uses the class database to enter the information they have gathered.

4. Analyze the data — When all of the class data have been entered, each team should decide on one main variable to explore. For example, they might want to focus just on the boys in the class, and then find out what characteristics and traits they have. When they find a pattern worth noting, they can create a printed report on it and share with the class.

5. Chart the data — Finally, they can present some of the data visually in chart form. They can post these charts on a bulletin board, and find answers (from the library and your science teacher) to questions the data raises about genetics.

National Standards:
NSTA Science Standards for Grades 9–12
• Science as inquiry
• Life science
• Science and technology

Required Resources:
Database software.

❖ ❖

Interdisciplinary Lessons Involving Science

❖ ❖

Title: Using Spreadsheets to Analyze Our Eating Habits
Grade Level: K–12
Source: Justice, B. (1996). Eating right? Fat chance! Teaching math and nutrition with spreadsheets. *Learning and Leading with Technology, 23*(8), 16–19.

Objectives/Purposes:

- Identify the food groups and daily recommended number of servings and serving sizes for each.
- Reinforce concepts of weights and measurements through food analysis.
- Create personal balanced diets.

In this activity, students use spreadsheets to do a combined study of nutrition, weights, and measurements. They enter data on a spreadsheet on how much they eat in each food category and how many calories and grams of fat they consume each day. They use these data to design their own daily balanced eating plan with the right number of servings from each food group and the correct calories and fat requirements for their age and activity levels.

Procedures:

1. Period 1 — Show the Food Pyramid poster to students, and give them each a copy of a smaller version of this display. Discuss what the pyramid shows. Help them focus on and analyze what they currently are eating by asking them to bring samples of food to class. Measure actual serving sizes of each food and ask them to determine how much of each type of food (e. g., cereal, butter, chicken) is in a single serving. Ask them to portion out the size serving they usually have and identify how many actual servings it is. (They may be surprised at the results of this comparison.)

2. Homework activity — Students pick a day to record on a record sheet all the food they eat in a 24-hour period in terms of food groups and servings. Remind them to include additions such as mayonnaise, sugar, and butter.

3. Periods 2–3 — Have students create a spreadsheet template on which they will enter the data they have collected. (NOTE: For younger students or to save time, the teacher can create this template.)

4. Period 4 — Have students enter the data onto the spreadsheet. Provide them with references from which they can calculate calories and fat grams.

5. Periods 5–6 — Students evaluate and analyze the results shown in the spreadsheet. Have them design a balanced diet for themselves with the appropriate servings of each food group, calories, and fat content. (Fat content should not exceed 30% of total calories.)

6. Assessment — Grade students on:
   - Accuracy of spreadsheet template (if they designed it)
   - Correctness of actual daily menu
   - Correctness of newly-designed, balanced daily menu
   - Participation and effort during labs

National Standards:
NSTA Science Standards for Grades 5–8 and 9–12
- Science as inquiry: Use appropriate tools and techniques to gather, analyze, and interpret data.
- Science in Personal and Social Perspectives: Personal health
NCTM Mathematics Standards for Grades K–4
- STANDARD #10: Measurement

Required Resources:
Spreadsheet software with template for food analysis; handouts on Food Pyramid; instructions for entering data; Typical Daily Menu worksheet.

◆ ◆

Title: Creating an Interactive Reference on Animals
Grade Level: 1–4
Source: Roscigno, S., and Shearin, L. (1995). Animals! Animals! Animals! *The Computing Teacher, 22* (7), 27–29.

Objectives/Purposes:
- Research information (e. g., homes, movement, body covering, eating) about animals.
- Create and deliver multimedia presentations based on research about animals.

In this activity, students will develop a multimedia stack to display their findings after a unit of study on animals. The result will be a product that organizes their work and allows them to access it more easily later.

Procedures:
1. Preparation — The class should spend a set amount of time, perhaps 45 minutes, each day reading, studying, and talking about animals; during which time they will become "animal experts." They can use a variety of materials ranging from books to videodiscs to gather information. They can do activities such as

classifying animals based on body coverings, comparing animals according to their characteristics, and even designing their own animals. While students attend to this work, the teacher should arrange folders on the multimedia screen so that students can store their work as they go along.

2. Initial research and work with multimedia tools — The teacher introduces 8 animals (or other appropriate number, depending on the number of students in the class) for students to research, divides the class into groups, and assigns an animal to each one. The teacher shows the class the title page in the multimedia stack; it should contain the five main topic headings that students should research: homes, movement, body covering, eating, and "fantastic facts." Then students are introduced to the tools they will use in the multimedia software. They should have an opportunity to experiment with the draw and paint tools and learn how to use the menus.

3. More research and multimedia development — Student groups should complete their research (they may need to visit the library/media center in groups). Available adult helpers can assist the children with reading difficult materials and locating information. Students will take notes on what they find and record answers to the research questions they are to address. After they complete the research, the group members should divide the responsibilities of writing a paragraph on each aspect of the animal they are studying. Available parent or other adult volunteers can be used to assist in editing and correcting the written summaries. After the work is edited, students begin entering it into the multimedia stack in the appropriate place. Then they select illustrations for their cards.

4. Product completion — To complete the products, the teacher can add selected videodisc clips from *Windows on Science* to the cards. A slideshow of all 8 animals can be used as an overview and introduction to the presentation.

5. Presentation — When the stack is completed, the students can explore the stack, reading and discussing the work on each animal. Parents could also be invited to an evening presentation to review the final product.

6. Extension Activities — Students may, in the future, use the Animals Stack as a reference tool. They can look up specific information on animals and complete an Animal Scavenger Hunt by looking for and completing short-answer exercises on the content.

National Standards:
NSTA Science Standards for K–4
- Science as inquiry
- Life science—Characteristics of organisms

NCTE English/Language Arts
- STANDARD #5: Students use a variety of technological and informational resources (e.g., libraries, networks, databases, video) to gather and synthesize information and to create and communicate knowledge.
- STANDARD #7: Students conduct research on issues and interests by generating ideas and questions and by posing problems.

Required Resources:
Computer lab with multimedia development software, such as *HyperStudio*; the *Windows on Science* videodisc.

◆ ◆

Title: Using Probeware to Integrate Mathematics and Science
Grade Level: 9–12
Source: Nadelson, L. (1994). Calibrating probeware: Making a line. *The Computing Teacher, 21*(6), 46–47.

Objectives/Purposes:
- Use the line equation intended for calibrating probeware/MBL (microcomputer-based laboratory) probes to explore mathematical concepts underlying the general linear equation $y = mx + b$.

Procedures:
1. The software that comes with probeware contains a line equation intended for calibrating the probes in the MBL probeware prior to collecting data on temperatures, voltage, and velocity. Students can use this software activity to explore mathematical concepts underlying the general linear equation $y = mx + b$ (where m = slope and b = the y-intercept).
2. Many different probeware setups call for the probe to be calibrated prior to using it for data collection. This process establishes a relationship between the input to the computer from the probe and the value that the measurement represents. The software gives instruction for how to do the calibration. For example, if the MBL is measuring voltage, the probe is calibrated by connecting it to AA battery that has been previously measured

by a multimeter and determined to be 1.5 volts
registers 215 counts for 1.5 volts.

3. The beginning point of 0 counts and the ending po
    a line. This line is used to calibrate the probe. Af
    calibrated, an equation is developed for the line
    1.5). Students sketch the graph of the line defined
    They may either use paper or graphing softwar
    values for "counts" given specific voltages using
    locating the value on the x-axis and finding the
    value for "counts." They use the general linear eq
    b to discuss the slope of the line as the rise (v
    between the two points) divided by the run (hor
    between the points).

4. The teacher has the students calculate the slop
    enter the value for the slope into the general linea
    do the final equation for the example calibra
    equation has been determined, have students ca
    for specific voltages. When the probe is ready t
    students bring in sample batteries to be tested.

National Standards:
NCTM Mathematics Standards for Grades 9–12
* STANDARD #4: Mathematical connections
* STANDARD #5: Algebra

NSTA Science Standards for Grades 9–12
* Science as inquiry
* Science and technology

Required Resources:
A probeware (microcomputer-based lab software + p
graphing software (if desired); and batteries.

❖ ❖

RESOURCES

Standards

Mathematics Standards from the National Council of Teachers of Mathematics (NCTM)
For a complete description of each standard, see NCTM's *Curriculum and Evaluation Standards for School Mathematics.*

Standards for Grades K–4

Standard #1:	Mathematics as Problem Solving
Standards #2:	Mathematics as Communication
Standard #3:	Mathematics as Reasoning
Standard #4:	Mathematical Connections
Standard #5:	Estimation
Standard #6:	Number Sense and Numeration
Standard #7:	Concepts of Whole Number Operations
Standard #8:	Whole Number Computation
Standard #9:	Geometry and Spatial Sense
Standard #10:	Measurement
Standard #11:	Statistics and Probability
Standard #12:	Fractions and Decimals
Standard #13:	Patterns and Relationships

Standards for Grades 5–8

Standard #1:	Mathematics as Problem Solving
Standard #2:	Mathematics as Communication
Standard #3:	Mathematics as Reasoning
Standard #4:	Mathematical Connections
Standard #5:	Number and Number Relationships
Standard #6:	Number Systems and Number Theory
Standard #7:	Computation and Estimation
Standard #8:	Patterns and Functions
Standard #9:	Algebra
Standard #10:	Statistics
Standard #11:	Probability
Standard #12:	Geometry
Standard #13:	Measurement

Standards for Grades 9–12

Standard #1:	Mathematics as Problem Solving
Standard #2:	Mathematics as Communication
Standard #3:	Mathematics as Reasoning
Standard #4:	Mathematical Connections

Standard #5:   Algebra
Standard #6:   Functions
Standard #7:   Geometry from a Synthetic Perspective
Standard #8:   Geometry from an Algebraic Perspective
Standard #9:   Trigonometry
Standard #10:   Statistics
Standard #11:   Probability
Standard #12:   Discrete Mathematics
Standard #13:   Conceptual Underpinnings of Calculus
Standard #14:   Mathematical Structure

English/Language Arts Standards from the National Council of Teachers of English (NCTE) and the International Reading Association (IRA)

For a complete statement and description of each standard, see NCTE's *Standards for the English Language Arts*

Standards for Grades K–12

1. "Students read a wide range of print and non-print texts to build an understanding of texts, of themselves, and of the cultures of the United States and the world ..."
2. "Students read a wide range of literature from many periods in many genres to build an understanding of the many dimensions... of human experience."
3. "Students apply a wide range of strategies to comprehend, interpret, evaluate, and appreciate texts..."
4. "Students adjust their use of spoken, written, and visual language to communicate effectively..."
5. "Students employ a wide range of strategies as they write and use different writing process elements appropriately..."
6. "Students apply knowledge of language structure, language conventions, media techniques, figurative language, and genre to create, critique, and discuss print and non-print texts."
7. "Students conduct research on issues and interests by generating ideas and questions, and by posing problems...[and] communicate their discoveries in ways that suit their purpose and audience."
8. "Students use a variety of technological and information resources...to gather and synthesize information and to create and communicate knowledge."
9. "Students develop an understanding of and respect for diversity in language use..."

10. "Students whose first language is not English make use of their first language to develop competency in the English language arts..."
11. "Students participate as knowledgeable, reflective, creative, and critical members of a variety of literacy communities."
12. "Students use spoken, written, and visual language to accomplish their own purposes." (*Standards for the English/Language Arts*, p. 3)

Social Science Standards from the National Council for the Social Studies (NCSS)

For a complete description of each standard, see NCSS's *Expectations of Excellence: Curriculum Standards for Social Studies*.

Standards for Grades K–12
    I. Culture
    II. Time, continuity, and Change
    III. People, Places, and Environments
    IV. Individual Development and Identity
    V. Individuals Groups, and Institutions
    VI. Power, Authority, and Governance
    VII. Production, Distribution, and Consumption
    VIII. Science, Technology, and Society
    IX. Global Connections
    X. Civic Ideals and Practice

Geography Standards from the Geography Standards Education Project

For a complete description of each standard, see National Geographic Research and Exploration's *Geography for Life: National Geography Standards, 1994.*

Standards for Grades K–12

The World in Spatial Terms
1. How to use maps and other geographic representations, tools, and technologies to acquire, process, and report information from a spatial perspective.
2. How to use mental maps to organize information about people, places, and environments in a spatial context.
3. How to analyze the spatial organization of people, places, and environments on Earth's surface.

Places and Regions
4. The physical and human characteristics of places.
5. That people create regions to interpret Earth's complexity.
6. How culture and experience influence people's perceptions of places and regions.

Physical Systems
7. The physical processes that shape the patterns of Earth's surface.
8. The characteristics and spatial distribution of ecosystems on Earth's surface.

Human Systems
9. The characteristics, distribution, and migration of human populations on Earth's surface.
10. The characteristics, distribution, and complexity of Earth's cultural mosaics.
11. The patterns and networks of economic interdependency on Earth's surface.
12. The processes, patterns, and functions of human settlement.
13. How the forces of cooperation and conflict among people influence the division and control of Earth's surface.

Environment and Society
14. How human actions modify the physical environment.
15. How physical systems affect human systems.
16. The changes that occur in the meaning, use, distribution, and importance of resources.

The Uses of Geography
17. How to apply geography to interpret the past.
18. How to apply geography to interpret the present and plan for the future. (back cover)

Standards for Civics and Government from the Center for Civic Education

For a complete description of each standard, and the questions under each heading, see the Center for Civic Education's *National Standards for Civics and Government*.

Standards for Grades K–4

I. *What Is Government and What Should It Do?*
This section includes questions on why a society needs a government, why societies have laws, how to evaluate those laws, and why it is important to limit the power of a government.

II. *What Are the Basic Values and Principles of American Democracy?*
This section includes questions on diversity in American society, the beliefs of the American people, and how the values of American society can be promoted.

III. *How Does the Government Established by the Constitution Embody the Purposes, Values, and Principles of American Democracy?*
This section includes questions about the United States Constitution, the responsibilities of state and local governments and the identity of the student's government representatives at all levels.

IV. *What Is the Relationship of the United States to other Nations and to World Affairs?*
This section includes questions on the organization and interaction of nations.

V. *What Are the Roles of the Citizen in American Democracy?*
This section includes questions on the rights and responsibilities of citizens, how to become a U. S. citizen, and American citizens' participation in their government. (National Standards for Civics and Government, pp. 13–14)

Standards for Grades 5–8

I. *What Are Civic Life, Politics, and Government?*
This section includes questions about various types of governments and definitions of the concepts of civic life, politics, and government.

II. *What Are the Foundations of the American Political System?*
This section deals with questions about American society and government, including its values, principles, and characteristics.

III. *How Does the Government Established by the Constitution Embody the Purposes, Values, and Principles of American Democracy?*
This section deals with the distribution of power among local, state, and federal governments. It also includes questions on the U. S. Constitution and how American citizens are permitted to participate in government.

IV. *What Is the Relationship of the United States to Other Nations and to World Affairs?*
This section deals with the political organization of the world and the influence of countries upon each other.

V. *What Are the Roles of the Citizen in American Democracy?*
This section deals with the rights and responsibilities of American citizens and ways they can participate in civic life. (National Standards for Civics and Government, pp. 43–44)

Standards for Grades 9–12

I. *What Are Civic Life, Politics, and Government?*
This section deals with information on the concepts of civic life, politics, and government. It also deals with questions about different types of governments and the reasons for a constitution for a government.

II. *What are the Foundations of the American Political System?*
This section deals with the characteristics, values, and principles of American society and government.

III. *How Does the Government Established by the Constitution Embody the Purposes, Values, and Principles of American Democracy?*
This section deals with the distribution of power among the levels and branches of government as defined in the United States Constitution. It also examines the opportunities American citizens have to participate in their government.

IV. *What Is the Relationship of the United States to Other Nations and to World Affairs?*
This section deals with the political organization of the world. It also deals with the influence the United States has on other nations, and the influence nations of the world have on each other.

V. *What Are the Roles of the Citizen in American Democracy?*
This section deals with the definition of citizenship, the rights and responsibilities of citizens of the United States, and how citizens can participate in civic life. It also contains questions dealing with the relationship of citizenship to the continuation of the American

democracy. (National Standards for Civics and Government, pp. 87–88)

Standards for Economic Education from the National Council on Economic Education (NCEE)

For a complete description of each standard, see NCEE's *Voluntary National Content Standards in Economics*.

Standards for grades K–12 (unless otherwise noted)

1. "Students will understand that productive resources are limited."
2. "Students will understand that effective decision making requires comparing the additional costs of alternatives with the additional benefits..."
3. "Students will understand that different methods can be used to allocate goods and services."
4. "Students will understand that people respond predictably to positive and negative incentives."
5. "Students will understand that voluntary exchange occurs only when all participating parties expect to gain."
6. "Students will understand that when individuals, regions, and nations specialize in what they can produce at the lowest cost and then trade with others, both production and consumption increase."
7. "Students will understand that markets exist when buyers and sellers interact..."
8. "Students will understand that prices send signals and provide incentives to buyers and sellers."
9. "Students will understand that competition among sellers lowers costs and prices, [and] Competition among buyers increases prices..."
10. "Students will understand that institutions evolve in market economies to help individuals and groups accomplish their goals."
11. "Students will understand that money makes it easier to trade, borrow, save, invest, and compare the value of goods and services."
12. "Students will understand that interest rates, adjusted for inflation, rise and fall to balance the amount saved with the amount borrowed..." (for grades 9–12)
13. "Students will understand that income, for most people, is determined by the market value of the productive resources they sell."

14. "Students will understand that entrepreneurs are people who take the risks of organizing productive resources to make goods and services."
15. "Students will understand that investment in factories, machinery, new technology, and in the health, education, and training of people can raise future standards of living."
16. "Students will understand that there is an economic role for government in a market economy whenever the benefits of a government policy outweigh its costs."
17. "Students will understand that costs of government policies sometimes exceed benefits." (for grades 9–12)
18. "Students will understand that a nation's overall level of income, employment, and prices are determined by the interaction of spending and production decisions made by all [members of] the economy." (for grades 5–8 & 9–12)
19. "Students will understand that unemployment imposes costs on individuals and nations."
20. "Students will understand that federal government budgetary policy and the Federal Reserve System's monetary policy influence the overall levels of employment, output and prices." (for grades 9–12) (*Voluntary National Content Standards in Economics*, pp. 2–41)

Science Education Standards from the National Research Council

For a complete description of each standard, see National Research Council's *National Science Education Standards*.

<u>Standards for Grades K–12 (these represent major areas of focus for science education)</u>

A. Science as Inquiry
B. Physical Science
C. Life Science
D. Earth and Space Science
E. Science and Technology
F. Science in Personal and Social Perspectives
G. History and Nature of Science Standards

Media Evaluation

When choosing software or other media to use in the classroom, it is important to choose material that is of good quality and is appropriate for the students and the lesson. The following questions serve as a guide for evaluating educational software, although the questions can also be applied to other technologies.

1. List the title of the software package.
2. List the publisher of the software package.
3. List the copyright date of the software package.
4. What is the suggested grade level for the package? Do you agree with that grade level? Why or why not?
5. Are there support materials to accompany the disk? If so, what are they and are they valuable?
6. Are there opportunities for user control? What are these opportunities? Do they help or hinder the program?
7. Is the program user friendly (easy to use, easy to read, free from bugs, etc.)?
8. Is the content accurate, free from errors, and free from bias?
9. What kind of feedback appears in the program? Is it appropriate? positive? immediate? Does it avoid reinforcing an incorrect response?
10. Are graphics and sound used in the program? If yes, are they appropriate? effective?
11. Does the program have branching capabilities — to various levels or new "chapters"? Does this help or hinder the program?
12. What kind, if any, of record keeping system is included with the program? What are the benefits of the system? What are the drawbacks of the system?
13. Is the software worth the price? Why or why not?
14. Does the software take advantage of the computer's capabilities?
15. Is the software appropriate for the intended audience and lesson?
16. What is your overall recommendation concerning this program?

Software Copyright Guidelines

(The following material comes, in part, from *Questions and Answers on Copyright for the Campus Community*, Copyright 1997, Association of American Publishers, National Association of College Stores, and Software Publishers Association.)

Copyright is the right granted by law to the creator of a work to control the use of the work created. This work may be published or unpublished, print or non-print. Only the owner of the copyright may reproduce, distribute or revise the work, or give the right to others to do so.

Copyright law does allow for some copying of materials under the "fair use" clause. Fair use allows the "limited use of portions of a copyrighted work without the permission for purposes such as criticism, comment, news reporting, teaching, scholarship, or research." (p. 4) These are only guidelines for fair use and are **not** to be interpreted as the legal definition of fair use; only the courts have the authority to determine if a particular use falls in this category.

In terms of software, the purchaser of software is permitted to make one copy for archival purposes only. This archival copy must be destroyed if the original disk is sold or given to someone else. Technically, a purchaser has not purchased the software, but rather has licensed the right to use it. Most software licenses allow for the use of the software on one machine at one time. Lab packs (multiple copies of the program bundled together) or a site license (the right to copy the software package on to a specified number of machines) are methods that educators can use to provide software for a number of machines in their schools. The publisher or distributor of a specific software title should be contacted to find out the policy regarding lab packs and site licenses.

Violation of the copyright law can result in civil and criminal penalties. The civil penalties are usually monetary in nature, and, in the cases of willful violation, can total up to $100,000.00 per work copied. Criminal penalties can result in fines and imprisonment.

For more information on software copyright and good software management, contact the Software Publisher's Association's website at http://www.spa.org

Web Resources

Learned Societies and Professional Organizations

◊ http://www.ncate.org
This is the website for NCATE (the National Council for the Accreditation of Teacher Education.

◊ http://www.cec.sped.org
This is the website for CEC (the Council for Exceptional Children). It includes links to professional standards, the ERIC Clearinghouse on Disabilities and Gifted Education, public policy links, and information on the organization.

◊ http://www.aect.org
This is the website for AECT (the Association for Educational Communications and Technology). It includes information on the organization, its affiliates, and professional development opportunities.

◊ http://www.ala.org
This is the website for the American Library Association (ALA). It includes links to news, education and professional development, web resources, and special events.

◊ http://www.ira.org
This is the website for IRA (the International Reading Association). It includes links to information about the organization, projects, and research.

◊ http://www.nctm.org
This is the website for NCTM (the National Council of Teachers of Mathematics). It includes general information from the organization as well as a link to case studies on using the NCTM Standards (http://www.nctm.org/case-studies/index.html)

◊ http://www.ncte.org
This is the website for NCTE (the National Council of Teachers of English). It includes general information from the organization as well as a link to ideas for teaching with technology (http://www.ncte.org/teach/technology)

◊ http://www.nsta.org
This is the website for NSTA (the National Science Teachers Association). It includes information on NSTA, its publications, programs, and projects as well as online science resources.

◊ http://www.nmsa.org
This is the website for the National Middle School Association (NMSA). It has information on the organization, links to the resource center, links to other relevant websites, and information on professional development.

◊ http://www.ncss.org
This is the website for NCSS (the National Council for the Social Studies). It has information about the organization, a discussion board, information on the classroom standards, and teaching resources. The site also includes links to associated groups and other Internet resources.

◊ http://www.nationalcouncil.org
This is the website for the NCEE (the National Council on Economic Education). It has information about the organization, the detailed standards for economic education, and other economics-related links.

Other Sites of Interest

◊ http://ericir.syr.edu
This is the website for the ERIC resource site. It includes access to lesson plans, the searchable ERIC database, and research documents.

◊ http://www.ed.gov
This is the website for the U.S. Department of Education. It includes a searchable database of Department of Education materials, information on programs, and research from the Department.

◊ http://www.nationalgeographic.com
This is National Geographic's website. It has links to many different topics on animals, land formations, and societies. It also includes atlases, information on the geography standards, and an interactive application of the standards.

◊   http://www.whitehouse.gov

This is the site for the White House. This site includes information on the President and Vice-President, an archive of presidential speeches and other documents, a virtual tour of the White House, and information on former presidents. This site also provides a link to the White House for Kids site.

◊   http://www.spa.org

This is the website for the Software Publisher's Association. It includes information on award-winning software as well as guidelines for following software copyright laws.

◊   http://nde4.nde.state.ne.us/TECHCEN/Software.html

This is a website from the Nebraska Department of Education that focuses on software preview and evaluation. It includes a number of links to software evaluation sites as well as other helpful, software-related sites.

◊   http://www.planetzoom.com/storybookpark.html

This is a website for student publications. Any student may submit stories or poems for publication on this site as long as the intended audience is children between the ages of 2 and 12. Students may also use this site to access a library of stories written by students and other authors.

◊   http://www.techlearning.com

This is the website from Technology and Learning magazine. It includes featured articles and a searchable database of educational software.

◊   http://www.capecod.net/schrockguide/index.htm

This is the website for Kathy Schrock's guide to the Internet. This site provides links to search engines and educational links arranged by topic. This is good starting point for new Internet users.

◊   http://www.whnt19.com/kidwx

This is Dan's Wild Wild Weather Page. It is managed by a meteorologist and contains information about various weather phenomena. It also provides answers to common weather questions, includes lesson plans for teachers, and access to free classroom resources.

◊ http://www.library.csi.cuny.edu/westweb
This website is devoted to the study of the history of the American West. It includes information on the various cultures that have been and are a part of the American West. It also includes links to teaching resources.

◊ http://tqjunior.advanced.org/3500
This website presents information on the animals of the Arctic region. It has links to information on specific animals, activities that can be completed by students, and a true story about a walrus hunt.

◊ http://www.cincyzoo.org
This is the website from the Cincinnati, Ohio, zoo. It allows users to learn about the animals that are at the zoo. There are also links to information about conservation, links especially for kids, and a link to educational ideas relating to the zoo and its animals.

◊ http://www.ldonline.org
This is the website for LD Online. This site serves as an interactive guide about learning disabilities for parents and teachers and students. It includes research on learning disabilities, art and writing from students, and a special feature that changes monthly.

◊ http://www.nyelabs.kcts.org
This is the website for Bill Nye the Science Guy's online lab. It has guides to the television episodes, demonstrations of the day, the science topic of the day, and links to search the web.

◊ http://www.artswire.org/kenroar/
This website contains information on art from the Art Education Association of Indiana. It provides art lessons and assessment ideas, the art site of the week, and the opportunity for students to submit their own art work for publication on the site.

◊ http://www.gale.com/gale/bhm/blackhm.html
This website focuses on African American History. It includes biographies of African American men and women, a timeline of events, relevant classroom literature, and a quiz on African American history.

Software Publisher Information

Listed below is the publisher information for the software products mentioned by title in the text. Contact the publisher for system requirements, price, and availability.

Note that most of these titles are also available through software stores and reseller catalogs.

The Amazing Writing Machine
    Broderbund Software
    500 Redwood Hwy
    PO Box 6125
    Novato, CA 94948-6125
    (800) 521-6263

Cartopedia: The Ultimate World Reference
    Dorling Kindersley Multimedia
    500 Redwood Hwy
    PO Box 6125
    Novato, CA 94948-6125
    (800) 521-6263

ClarisWorks
    Claris Corporation
    5201 Patrick Henry Drive
    Box 58168
    Santa Clara, CA 95052-8168
    (800) 544-8554

Compton's Multimedia Encyclopedia
    The Learning Company/Compton's Home Interactive
    6493 Kaiser Drive
    Fremont, CA 94555
    (800) 227-5609

Easy Graph II
    Houghton Mifflin Interactive
    120 Beacon Street
    Somerville, MA 02143
    (617) 503-4800

Exploring Tables and Graphs
>Optimum Resources, Inc.
>5 Hilteck Lane
>Hilton Head, SC 29926
>(803) 689-8000

Flight Simulator
>Microsoft Corporation
>One Microsoft Way
>Redmond, WA 98052
>(800) 426-9400

Geometer Sketchpad
>Key Curriculum Press
>PO Box 2304
>Berkeley, CA 94702
>(800) 995-MATH

The Graph Club
>Tom Snyder Productions
>80 Coolidge Hill Road
>Watertown, MA 02172
>(800) 342-0236

HyperCard
>Apple Computer, Inc.
>1 Infinite Loop
>Cupertino, CA 95014
>(408) 996-1010

HyperStudio
>Roger Wagner
>1050 Pioneer Way, Suite P
>El Cajon, CA 92020
>(800) 497-3778

Kid Pix
>Broderbund Software
>500 Redwood Hwy
>PO Box 6125
>Novato, CA 94948-6125
>(800) 521-6263

Kid Works
>
> Davidson and Associates
> 19840 Pioneer Ave.
> Torrance, CA 90503
> (800) 545-7677

Managing Lifestyles
>
> Sunburst Communications
> 101 Castleton Street
> Pleasantville, NY 10570
> (800) 321-7511

MapQuest (with TripQuest)
>
> MapQuest Publishing Group - Denver
> 1730 Blake Street, Suite 310
> Denver, CO 80202
> (303) 312-0200
>
> MapQuest Publishing Group - Mountville
> 3710 Hempland Road
> Mountville, PA 17554
> (717) 285-8500
>
> Also, see http://www.mapquest.com

Microsoft Encarta
>
> Microsoft Corporation
> One Microsoft Way
> Redmond, WA 98052
> (800) 426-9400

Microsoft Excel
>
> Microsoft Corporation
> One Microsoft Way
> Redmond, WA 98052
> (800) 426-9400

Microsoft PowerPoint
>
> Microsoft Corporation
> One Microsoft Way
> Redmond, WA 98052
> (800) 426-9400

Microsoft Word
>Microsoft Corporation
>One Microsoft Way
>Redmond, WA 98052
>(800) 426-9400

MicroWorlds Project Builder
>Logo Computer Systems, Inc. (LCSI)
>PO Box 162
>Highgate Springs, VT 05460
>(800) 321-5646

Muppet Math
>Sunburst Communications
>101 Castleton Street
>Pleasantville, NY 10570
>(800) 321-7511

Science Toolkit (probeware)
>Broderbund Software
>500 Redwood Hwy
>PO Box 6125
>Novato, CA 94948-6125
>(800) 521-6263

Survival Math
>Sunburst Communications
>101 Castleton Street
>Pleasantville, NY 10570
>(800) 321-7511

Windows on Science videodisc series:
>Optical Data Corporation
>512 Means St. NW
>Suite 100
>Atlanta, GA 30318
>(800) 201-7103

References and Suggested Readings

Curriculum and evaluation standards for school mathematics. (1989). Reston, VA: The National Council of Teachers of Mathematics.

Dockterman, D. A. (1997). *Great teaching in the one computer classroom* (4th ed.). Watertown, MA: Tom Snyder Productions.

Dynneson, T. L. & Gross, R. E. (1995). *Designing effective instruction for secondary social studies.* Upper Saddle River, NJ: Merrill/Prentice Hall.

Ebenezer, J. V. & Connor, S. (1998). *Learning to teach science: A model for the 21st century.* Upper Saddle River, NJ: Merrill/Prentice Hall.

Expectations of excellence: Curriculum standards for the social studies. (1994). Washington, D.C.: National Council for the Social Studies.

Geography Education Standards Project. (1994). *Geography for life: National geography standards.* Washington, D.C.: National Geographic Research and Exploration.

Herrell, A. L., & Fowler, J. P., Jr. (1998). *Camcorder in the classroom: Using the videocamera to enliven curriculum.* Upper Saddle River, NJ: Merrill/Prentice Hall.

Howe, A. C., & Jones, L. (1998). *Engaging children in science* (2nd ed.). Upper Saddle River, NJ: Merrill/Prentice Hall.

Maxim, G. W. (1995*). Social studies and the elementary school child* (5th ed.). Upper Saddle River, NJ: Merrill/Prentice Hall.

NCATE approved curriculum guidelines. (1995). Washington, D.C.: National Council for Accreditation of Teacher Education.

National Council for Economic Education. (n.d.). *Voluntary national content standards in economics.* [on-line] Available: http://www.economicsamerica.org.bigtext.html

National Research Council. (1996). *National science education standards.* Washington, D.C.: National Academy Press.

National standards for civics and government. (1994). Calabasas, CA: Center for Civic Education.

Newby, T. J., Stephich, D. A., Lehman, J. D., & Russell, J. D. (1996). *Instructional technology for teaching and learning: Designing instruction, integrating computers, and using media.* Upper Saddle River, NJ: Merrill/Prentice Hall.

Questions and answers on copyright for the campus community. (1997). Oberlin, OH: National Association of College Stores.

Reutzel, D. R., & Cooter, R. B., Jr. (1996). *Teaching children to read: From basals to books* (2nd ed.). Upper Saddle River, NJ: Merrill/Prentice Hall.

Robyler, M. D. (1999). *Integrating technology across the curriculum: A database of strategies and lesson plans.* [CD-ROM] Upper Saddle River, NJ: Merrill/Prentice Hall.

Roblyer, M. D., Edwards, J. & Havriluk, M. A. (1997). *Integrating educational technology into teaching.* Upper Saddle River, NJ: Merrill/Prentice Hall.

Simonson, M. R. & Thompson, A. D. (1996). *Educational computing foundations* (3rd ed.). Upper Saddle River, NJ: Merrill/Prentice Hall.

Standards for English/language arts. (1996). Urbana, IL: National Council of Teachers of English.

Tompkins, G. E. (1998). *Language arts: Content and teaching strategies* (4th ed.). Upper Saddle River, NJ: Merrill/Prentice Hall.

Tompkins, G. E. (1997*). Literacy for the 21st century: A balanced approach* (2nd ed.). Upper Saddle River, NJ: Merrill/Prentice Hall.